DELIVERANCE

AN END TIMES MINISTRY THE CHURCH CAN NO LONGER IGNORE

By

Deliverance Evangelist Peter Valenzuela

EXPAND MY KINGDOM

Evangelistic Association

DELIVERANCE

An End Times Ministry The Church Can No Longer Ignore

Printed in the United States of America

By

Deliverance Evangelist Peter Valenzuela

EXPAND MY KINGDOM Evangelistic Association

ISBN: 9798884263857
Imprint: Independently published

TABLE OF CONTENTS

EVANGELIST PETER VALENZUELA

ACKNOWLEDGEMENTS

I would have never imagined I would be the author of a book, but the Holy Spirit had given me the idea and I remember telling myself I could not do it. Then God spoke to a friend within a few months, who told me, 'I would write a book' She boldly declared that God was telling me I would do it. I, therefore, decided to move forward and began this task, which was only accomplished by the divine enablement of the Holy Spirit and his GRACE! So, I want to thank, first and foremost the Holy Spirit that was the game changer in my life in 2022 and 2023! I also want to honor my Mother and dedicate this book to her *'Martha Valenzuela, August 14th, 1950 – April 1, 2022.'* My sweet Mom was a wonderful, Mighty woman of God that never gave up on me; when I was addicted to heroin, cocaine; and miserably bound by Sin! I remember her telling me the most difficult things I needed to hear, and I will never forget that!

FOREWORD

Welcome to a world the mainstream churches have long forgotten. The rise of Satan's power cannot be denied or overlooked anymore. The Spirit of the LORD is raising up a deliverance revival as the standard against Satan's takeover of the U.S. Read with caution and a sense of urgency as Bro. Peter Valenzuela leads you in your deliverance journey and how to respond to the War of the Kingdom of Darkness in these last days. Welcome to the future.

Michael W. Smith, M.S., C.R.C., C.D.M.S./R.

Director HardcoreChristianity.Com and the Arizona Deliverance Center, Phoenix, AZ.

EVANGELIST PETER VALENZUELA

PREFACE

After my initial born again experience in 2008, when I was radically born again through a glorious encounter with the divine Master Jesus Christ, I have never been the same! Up until 2008 my life was plagued by death, sickness, addiction, fear, witchcraft, rejection, and shame! My life was the manifestation of *John 10:10 "the thief comes to steal, kill and destroy"* Deep down in my heart, I wanted to believe in God and always hoped there was a God, but the traumatic and negative experiences in my life led me to atheism; unbelief and doubt when the question of a loving God would come up. The greatest day of my life was when I saw JESUS face to face! I immediately became a follower and a lover of JESUS in 5 seconds when he revealed himself to me! After calling on his 'NAME' according to *Jeremiah 33:3, 'Call unto me, and I will answer thee, and show thee great and mighty things, which thou knowest not.'* What would ensue in the next couple of years leading up to my deliverance in 2011 was an onslaught of the satanic kingdom to derail, discourage, wickedly influence and destroy the call of God on my life. If Satan has admittedly lost you from his clutches and his kingdom, his next plan is to keep you from accomplishing and fulfilling God's high calling and purpose for your life. The discipleship program where I met JESUS did not train me in spiritual-warfare or prepare me to take an offensive approach as a believer, and I was falling victim to Satan out of ignorance. I was never told that every contract I made with Satan was being used against me still, even though I was born again! And every lie I believed was a spiritual tie with the kingdom of darkness that needed to be renounced and broken off my mind to walk in the freedom Christ wrought for me! So, I was struggling emotionally, mentally, and financially and my marriage at the time was falling apart. I would spend hours memorizing scripture and hours in prayer. Although I grew as a believer, it seemed like the enemy had the upper hand! No one ever warned me about demons, so eventually, the Holy Spirit had to step in and reveal my spiritual problems and how Satan had gained legal rights into my soul. He showed me through ancestral sin, family dysfunction, drug addiction, sexual sin, negative inner vows, generational curses, trauma, the occult and spiritual contracts that I made with Satan out of ignorance, were allowing the unclean spirits to inflict havoc in my life! My ex-wife Holly in 2010 discovered a deliverance ministry called the house of healing. She came home one evening saying, 'I think I need deliverance from demons' I was upset and proudly responded, come here, I'll get those devils out of you. I prayed for her and I remember her demons manifesting and her admitting something in her hated me; I quickly realized I was completely helpless; weak and unsuccessful praying against what she was battling in her soul. Eventually, I went to the house of healing and realized I was also heavily infected by evil spirits as well. *After believing that Christians could not have demons and actually being mad that God would allow this; I realized God did not allow this demonic influence in my life, I invited Satan in and God in his grace was revealing this to me; to train and deliver me for a purpose in these end times!* To make a long story short, the Holy Spirit always put a book in my hands for different seasons of training in my life. In this season of my life, he placed 'Pigs in the Parlor' in my hands by Frank and Ida Mae Hammond. They were a wonderful deliverance couple that God had used mightily in the '80s and '90s. In 1980 Hammond founded 'the Children's Bread ministry' with his wife, Ida Mae Hammond. In this

wonderful book, the Holy Spirit had given Ida Mae
a revelation of schizophrenia and mental illness.
When I was reading it, the Holy Spirit spoke to my
spirit and highlighted the pages of the book,
revealing what was wrong with me all these years!
And how the network of demons had infiltrated my
soul through a strongman of rejection and rebellion.
The schizophrenia revelation Ida Mae received
from the Holy Spirit was exactly what I needed to
know and was enough for me to begin my pursuit of
deliverance! That is why I have chosen deliverance
as the topic of my first book, because of the urgency
and importance for the believer to be trained
properly and receive what God the Father paid such
a high price for 'the life and shed blood of his Son'
for his people to take hold of deliverance and fulfill
the call of God without Satan thwarting and
derailing their lives! *The main problem, the
deep-seated hurts, the pain, the bad habits,
the addictions, and the evil circumstances
that are repeated in our lives are the result of
unclean spirits. Until we recognize that, and
confront them by the authority we have in the
Christ, the problems, the evil circumstances,
the trials, and the demonic storms will
continue!*

INTRODUCTION

My name is bro Peter Valenzuela, and I want to thank you for reading this book about the controversial Ministry of deliverance started by the divine Master himself Jesus Christ 2000 years ago! In Mark 16:17-18, he commanded all believers to cast out demons, not some, not a few, not pastors and evangelists, but ALL BELIEVERS! *Mark 16:17-18 NKJV 'And these signs will follow those who believe: In My name they will Cast out demons; they will speak with new tongues; they will take up serpents; and if they drink anything deadly, it will by no means hurt them; they will lay hands on the sick, and they will recover"* Deliverance is the complete eradication and destruction of the satanic kingdom by the KINGDOM of God, breaking it into pieces; plundering hell, and populating heaven! *'Daniel 2:44 'And in the days of these kings shall the God of heaven set up a kingdom, which shall never be destroyed: and the kingdom shall not be left to other people, but it shall break in pieces and consume all these*

13

kingdoms, and it shall stand for ever.
Deliverance is truly walking in the New Creation Paul spoke about. **2 Cor 5:17 NKJV 'Therefore if any man be in Christ, he is a New Creation: old things are passed away; behold, all things are become new'** Years ago, when I received the call into the Ministry of deliverance, I had a divine dream and God showed me that his LOVE is the foundation for deliverance and that once the devils are casted out or driven out, we become the New Creation! In my dream, I was ministering to a woman involved in new age witchcraft. I immediately began to pray for her and as I was speaking to her, *'the glorious LOVE of God being released through my mouth was delivering her!* It was a life changing dream, that I always remember and ponder when I struggle because it keeps me going hard after the WILL of God in my life, now we can understand **1 John 4:18 'There is no fear in love; but perfect love casteth out fear: because fear hath torment. He that feareth is not made perfect in love.'** After a radical deliverance had taken place by the LOVE of God being released through my mouth, I then introduced her to the end times Church for protection, fellowship, and discipleship!

It was then that the Holy Spirit revealed to me in the dream that she was now the *'New Creation'* and that only after we had cast out the demons do we become the manifestation of 2 Cor 5:17! In Acts 26:18, Paul stated that everyone needs to be turned from darkness to light or receive some level of deliverance! ***'Acts 26:18 NKJV 'To open their eyes, and to turn them from darkness to light, and from the power of Satan unto God, that they may receive forgiveness of sins, and inheritance among them which are sanctified by faith that is in me'.*** It is my assignment by divine enablement and GRACE to teach, train and equip believers to EXPAND the KINGDOM of God by the wiping out and destruction of Satan's kingdom, and that's what we will focus on in this book! ***Matt 12:28 'But if I cast out devils by the Spirit of God, then the kingdom of God is come unto you'*** We will explain what deliverance is, how to obtain it and practically minister it to others! *After careful review, practical activation, and applying the principles taught in this book, you will be an expert in the area of 'healing the sick' and 'casting out devils, which I believe is the highest calling on the earth!*

I hope this book blesses you and equips you for the wonderful, satisfying and exhilarating end time ministry of deliverance or the "casting out of demon' Mandated by the divine Master Jesus Christ himself! *Matthew 10:8 TLB 'Heal the sick, raise the dead, cure the lepers, and CAST OUT DEMONS. Give as freely as you have received!* Christ never sent anyone to preach the GOSPEL of the KINGDOM without first authorizing them to cast out devils! It is unbiblical to preach the gospel and not confront devils and destroy Satan's kingdom! *Mark 6:7 KJV 'And he called unto him the twelve, and began to send them forth by two and two; and gave them power over unclean spirits;* See this same verse in the Young's literal translation *Mark 6:7 'And he doth call near the twelve, and he began to send them forth two by two, and he was giving them power over the unclean spirits'.*

Chapter 1

MANIFESTING AND ESTABLISHING THE KINGDOM OF GOD

TWO OPPOSING KINGDOMS

In order to understand deliverance and spiritual warfare, we need to realize there are two kingdoms in operation on the earth today. Not natural kingdoms like Mexico and Canada, they are invisible spiritual kingdoms! The KINGDOM of God and the kingdom of Satan. In Matthew Chapter 12 'JESUS was casting out devils, and the Pharisees accused him of casting out demons by Beelzebub, the ruler of the demons. Let us look at verses 26 and 28 in the NKJV *'if Satan casts out Satan, he is divided against himself. How then will his kingdom stand?* In verse 26, 'Jesus stated Satan has a kingdom, and in verse 28, Jesus discusses the KINGDOM of God. *'But if I cast out demons by the Spirit of God, surely the kingdom of God has come upon you'*

Satan, unclean spirits or demons, invisible spirit beings or persons without bodies represent the kingdom of Satan! JEHOVAH the great Hebrew God, Jesus Christ, the Holy Spirit, the Holy angels and his Servants the end-times Church represent the KINGDOM of God. The visible collision of the KINGDOM of God and the satanic kingdom is brought out into the open by the driving out of demons! The fact that the Church can drive out demons proves the SUPREMACY of the KINGDOM of God over Satan's defeated kingdom! That is why Satan hates and opposes the deliverance ministry, because it brings out into the open things he would rather keep secret! In this verse the apostle makes this point clear, that there is two kingdoms in operation on the earth! ***Colossians 1:12-13 TLB 'And always thankful to the Father who has made us fit to share all the wonderful things that belong to those who live in the Kingdom of light. For he has rescued us out of the darkness and gloom of Satan's kingdom and brought us into the Kingdom of his dear Son.*** Here in Matt 13:38 'Jesus discussed the children of the KINGDOM and children of Satan'

Matthew 13:38 KJV 'The field is the world; the good seed are the children of the kingdom; but the tares are the children of the wicked one' Here JESUS explains the difference between both kingdoms and what the KINGDOM of God does in our lives.' *John 10:10 KJV 'the enemy comes to steal, kill & destroy (the kingdom of darkness) but I come that you might have life and have it more abundantly' (the KINGDOM of God).*

THE CLASH BETWEEN TWO KINGDOMS

Matthew 12:22-23 NKJ 'Then one was brought to Him who was demon-possessed, blind and mute; and He healed him, so that the blind and mute man both spoke and saw. And all the multitudes were amazed and said, "Could this be the Son of David? We see here that Satan's kingdom is evil and those captured by him are held in bondage. This mans wretched blindness and muteness were due to demonic

EVANGELIST PETER VALENZUELA

chains! The POWER and DOMINANCE of the KINGDOM of God is reflected in the man's healing! As soon as KING JESUS came on the scene the chains of sickness were demolished by the glorious Christ! When we get the revelation of the KINGDOM of God our lives shift toward freedom! That is what the KINGDOM of God is; Satan does not mind you hearing sermons that are focused on self and your best life! He is ok with you hearing about prosperity and salvation, three worship songs, a 20 min sermonette and then hitting the lunch buffet before the Baptist by 1pm every Sunday! *He is only afraid of one message, the KINGDOM message!* The revelation of KING JESUS; the revelation of the KINGDOM of God; revealing the KING and what he did for us! Exposing and displaying the destruction and defeat of the satanic kingdom! Revealing the IDENTITY of the people of the KINGDOM and revealing the promises the KING died to provide! Satan fears you getting this revelation of the KINGDOM so much so; that when you hear it, he will immediately try and snatch it up! *He will fight you on reading this book, because it exposes his utter-defeat and proclaims your VICTORY in the Christ and his KINGDOM!*

Matthew 13:19 KJV 'When anyone hears the word of the kingdom and does not understand it, then the wicked one comes and snatches away what was sown in his heart' Disciple of Christ, *may you get the WORD of the KINGDOM in your heart with understanding and do whatever it takes to keep the WORD and be a DOER of it! Do not give the wicked one any right to steal the WORD from your heart!*

JESUS CAME TO RESTORE UNTO US THE KINGDOM OF GOD

Luke 22:29 NKJV 'And I appoint unto you a kingdom, as my Father hath appointed unto me' HE DIDN'T COME JUST TO DIE FOR OUR SINS AND GET US INTO HEAVEN ONE DAY! That was a means to accomplish his end goal and priority! JESUS did not come to establish a religion, a ceremonial, dead boring, repetitive halleluiah club with no freedom! JESUS did not bring any separate or individual denominations; JESUS did not bring a self-help, quick-fix short-cut! JESUS came to redeem what

Adam lost and bring you the KINGDOM of God, in all of its POWER, ANOINTING, VICTORY, GRACE, TRANSFORMATION, PROSPERITY and AUTHORITY! ***Luke 12:32 KJV 'Fear not, little flock; for it is your Father's good pleasure to give you the Kingdom'*** The Fathers purpose in his Son was to redeem what Adam forfeited to the enemy! ***Matthew 25:34 KJV 'Then the King will say to those on His right hand, 'Come, you blessed of My Father, inherit the Kingdom prepared for you from the foundation of the world'*** The Greek word for KINGDOM is 'Basilea', which literally means 'Royal power and dominion' In order to be successful in deliverance we need to know what the KINGDOM of God is! The KINGDOM of God is the RULE and REIGN of God; it is a territory governed by God. It is a natural and spiritual realm where the will of God, the plans of God, the purposes of God, the promises of God, the desires of God, and the WORD of God are fulfilled in our lives! The KINGDOM of God is where the FIRE of God, the GRACE of God, the MERCY of God, the ANOINTING of God, the AUTHORITY of God, the POWER of God, the PRESENCE of God, the WORD of God, and the LOVE of God is

ESTABLISHED in our lives! The KING of the KINGDOM, Jesus Christ wants his people to live in the KINGDOM of God, rout devils, destroy, expose, shame; bruise, trample, tread-upon, and crush with your feet, the kingdom of darkness! Now you can understand these two declarations Christ made! ***Matthew 6:33 KJV But seek ye first the kingdom of God, and his righteousness; and all these things shall be added unto you'*** We will never casually or accidentally bump into the KINGDOM of God, but rather we need to seek it wholeheartedly, boldly and powerfully pursue it! 'zeteo' is the Greek word for seek, which literally means 'to seek in order to find, to seek in order to find out by thinking and meditating,' to require, and demand. So we learn from this scripture, we are to *'Seek, meditate on, think about, and find the KINGDOM of God, as we demand every promise KING JESUS died to provide us!* ***Matthew 11:12 KJV And from the days of John the Baptist until now the kingdom of heaven suffereth violence, and the violent take it by force'*** The Greek word for force is 'harpazo' here which literally means to seize, to carry off by force, to claim for oneself eagerly.

So, we learn from this scripture; *'We take the KINGDOM of God by force, to claim for oneself eagerly and carry off by force the promises of God, as we seize and take hold of the KINGDOM of God.'*

KING JESUS IS A DELIVERER

I was born again on Jan 26th 2008, as a Christian I was powerfully delivered in 2011. I had a lot of spiritual problems after my initial born again experience and after the Holy Spirit revealed to me that I needed deliverance, JESUS broke demonic chains off my mind, my life, my soul, and my body and drove the devils out! *Today I have a sound mind, VICTORY, PEACE, and JOY! And I am not ashamed of what JESUS did for me!* When people are ashamed of what JESUS died for his people to receive which is 'deliverance from devils' they do not retain deliverance! That is pride at work causing people to be ashamed of what they have received from the Christ and the glorious work of the Holy Spirit. I will tell it to the world until the day I die; 'I was powerfully delivered from evil spirits by the glorious Christ! *Luke 13:32 KJV*

'And He said to them, "Go, tell that fox, 'Behold, I cast out demons" One evening in my backyard, we were having a wonderful fellowship with the body of Christ and deliverance broke out! The Holy Spirit quickened me and said 'begin to cast-out devils' what started off as a fellowship and bonfire, ended up being a magnificent deliverance session with two beautiful couples being wonderfully delivered by Jesus Christ! Sadly, one of the couples decided that what had happened was not ok with them and refused to come around anymore because of what others witnessed. Sin invites devils in to steal, kill and destroy, when demons come out it will get strangely uncomfortable and ugly; that's ok, because sin is also ugly! We should never feel ashamed of receiving the Children's bread that JESUS paid a terrible price for us to receive! I have never seen that couple again because the enemy led them astray and their dignity there was shattered. You can't have both, 'dignity and deliverance' release your dignity for a season and obtain your deliverance! *Psalms 18:48 'He delivers me from my enemies. You also lift me up above those who rise against me; You have delivered me from the violent man.* I was so happy the day I received

deliverance from the divine Master Jesus Christ! After coughing up demons for three hours one night, my eyes looked like I was beaten with a baseball bat, my eyes were bruised and swollen when the devils were renounced, their power broken and the demons driven out. I felt so light and super blessed because the KINGDOM of God had come upon me! The KINGDOM of God was manifested in my life and destroyed the kingdom of darkness, and I have never been the same! ***Luke 11:20 'But if I cast out demons with the finger of God, surely the kingdom of God has come upon you.*** Life has not been easy since then, but it has been a wonderful, continual process of gaining freedom; 'one spiritual inch after another' with training, preparation, equipping, and hands-on experience! God the Holy Spirit preparing me for the CALL of God on my life! And because I received deliverance, now I can help others receive it. ***Matthew 10:7-8 KJV 'And as ye go, preach, saying, The kingdom of heaven is at hand. Heal the sick, cleanse the lepers, raise the dead, cast out devils: freely ye have received, freely give.*** Deliverance is a distinctive ministry of the Jewish Messiah! All leaders, patriarchs, prophets, seers, priests, and judges, from Moses,

Samson, Daniel, and Elijah to John the Baptist, never cast out demons before! ***Psalms 59:1 'Deliver me from my enemies, O my God; protect me from those who rise against me'*** The KING of the JEWS, the ANOINTED-ONE of JEHOVAH, the Christos in Greek (the Anointed One, Messiah, the Christ) would be the first to cast out demons! And he commanded his followers to do the same works he did! KING Jesus Christ is a deliverer! ***John 14:12-14 KJV verily, I say unto you, He that believeth on me, the works that I do shall he do also; and greater works than these shall he do; because I go unto my Father. And whatsoever ye shall ask in my name, that will I do, that the Father may be glorified in the Son. If ye shall ask any thing in my name, I will do it.***

THE ORDER OF THE KINGDOM IS DELIVERANCE FIRST THEN DISCIPLESHIP!

EVERYONE WANTS TO FOCUS ON
DISCIPLESHIP AND LEAVE DELIVERANCE
OUT; but when you leave out the FULL GOSPEL
of the KINGDOM, which includes the 'casting out
of demons' we end up with tormented and troubled
Christians that Satan derails and hinders from
successfully obtaining the plans and purposes of
God. Mary Magdalene heard the gospel of the
KINGDOM, she then received deliverance! She
was then a disciple of the Christ and became the
New Creation! 'Later she was the first to hear about
the resurrection at the tomb by the ANGEL of the
LORD! *Luke 8:1-2 KJV 'Now it came to
pass, afterward, that He went through
every city and village, preaching and
bringing the glad tidings of the
kingdom of God. And the twelve
were with Him, and certain women
who had been healed of evil spirits
and infirmities—Mary called
Magdalene, out of whom had come
seven demons.'* After receiving the Christ, new
believers will be on cloud nine, but then problems
arise, and real struggles take place! Storms,
affliction, challenges, trials, and evil circumstances
arise! Soon many get discouraged because they are
not advancing and making progress; it is at that

point when deliverance is necessary! If it does not happen, we become unhealthy believers and deformed Christians stuck in demonic derailment, deception, and frequent spiritual storms! ***2 Cor 5:17 KJV 'Therefore if any man be in Christ, he is a new creature: old things are passed away; behold, all things are become new'*** The revelation here is that the New Creation is "In Christ" they didn't just say a prayer and accept Christ, they live in the Christ, they RADICALLY OBEY the Christ, they LOVE the Christ, there submitted to the Christ! And because they do what God requires them to do; now they are in a position to tell Satan what he must do! You will boldly say, devil you can't do that anymore; I am resisting you in the faith now!' ***1 Peter 5:9 KJV 'Whom resist steadfast in the faith, knowing that the same afflictions are accomplished in your brethren that are in the world.*** The Greek word for resist here is "anthistemi" which literally means 'one is setting himself against' withstanding and opposing another' from this scripture, we learn *'We resist, withstand, oppose; and stand against Satan; all of his lies and influence; knowing your brothers in Christ are overcoming the same afflictions.'*

DELIVERANCE IS THE KINGDOM OF GOD IN ACTION!

Matthew 12:28 KJV 'But if I cast out devils by the Spirit of God, then the kingdom of God is come unto you.' One morning in 2011, after praying in the spirit for about an hour, I fell under a trance, with my eyes open and all of a sudden, the ANGEL of the LORD sent from the presence of ALMIGHTY God was standing in my living room! And the call and mandate came forth concerning the KINGDOM of God! *Luke 11:20 KJV 'But if I with the finger of God cast out devils, no doubt the kingdom of God is come upon you."* I am here to declare to you today; the priority of KING JESUS is the EXPANSION of his KINGDOM by the destruction and diminishing of the satanic kingdom! And to redeem what Adam lost. He came to manifest and display the superiority and supremacy of the KINGDOM of God over Satan's kingdom! Not to bring a boring dead religion, with rules and regulations, and strict denominations that operate in legalism and carnality. With churches competing with other churches, and pastors being filled with pride, focused on their programs, finances, and ministries that need little help from God to be successful; but his eternal KINGDOM and the increase of it by preaching the KINGDOM of God! ***Luke 16:16 KJV The law and the prophets were until John: since that time, the Kingdom of God is preached and every man presseth into it'*** 'Presseth into is the Greek word 'Biazo' which literally means to use force, to apply force, to inflict violence on' So here we learn from this scripture '*In the New Testament we only preach the KINGDOM of God! And we use FORCE, and repeatedly apply force; as we inflict violence on Satan's kingdom, utterly eradicating and destroying his influence in our lives; FORCING him to GO!*'

THE DELIVERANCE MINISTRY BRINGS OUT SATAN TO AN OPEN MANIFEST DEFEAT

1 Corinthians 4:20 KJV 'For the KINGDOM of God is not in word, but in POWER.' Paul said the KINGDOM of God is the power of God displayed! And when the KINGDOM of God is displayed and established; devils flee; devils bow, devils get routed, devils are embarrassed, because the Holy Ghost is the Master of all evil spirits and he is living inside of you! And now JESUS will destroy, demolish, trample and conquer every devil in your life! ***Matthew 9:35 'And Jesus went about all the cities and villages, teaching in their synagogues, and preaching the gospel of the kingdom, and healing every sickness and every disease among the people.*** JESUS the KING of the KINGDOM made it clear, that the end times Ministry of deliverance would establish his eternal KINGDOM on the earth; restoring what Adam lost! ***Luke 9:1-2 KJV 'Then he called his twelve disciples together, and gave them power and authority over all devils, and to cure diseases. And he sent them to preach the kingdom of God, and to heal the sick'*** Notice in the gospels JESUS only preached the KINGDOM of God, not salvation, deliverance, divine healing, or prosperity. ***Matthew 4:23-24 "And Jesus went about all Galilee, teaching in their synagogues, and preaching the gospel of the KINGDOM,*** *and healing all manner of sickness and all manner of disease among the people. Then His fame went throughout all Syria; and they brought to Him all sick people who were afflicted with various diseases and torments, and those who were demon-possessed, epileptics, and paralytics; and He healed them'* The kingdom of darkness operates like the cockroach kingdom, always hiding in the dark! The KINGDOM of God will expose what the enemy does to people and display its dominance, strength and POWER over darkness through anointed end-time ambassadors and representatives of the KINGDOM of God.

2 Corinthians 5:20 'Now then, we are ambassadors for Christ, as though God were pleading through us: we implore you on Christ's behalf, be reconciled to God' An ambassador is someone sent by a GOVT as its official representative to a foreign country; a representative of a government appointed for a special assignment! A KINGDOM ambassador establishes the KINGDOM of God on the earth! Christ ambassadors represent Heavens GOVT and it provides all their needs!

The **KINGDOM** provides their house, pays their mortgage and provides their transportation! The ambassador of the **KINGDOM** of God does not have his or her own opinion; when asked about how they feel about a certain topic (abortion, same-sex marriage), they always refer to the constitution of the government or the **WORD** of the **KINGDOM**! *You are an end-time ambassador sent by heavens GOVT to your region to influence that territory with the Culture of the KINGDOM and EXPAND the KINGDOM of God in your region.*

NOTES:

_____

_____

_____

_____

_____

_____

_____

_____

_____

_____

_____

_____

Chapter 2

SATAN'S ETERNAL DEFEAT

<u>CHRIST HAS ALREADY DEFEATED SATAN AND ALL PRINCIPALITIES AND POWERS!</u>

THROUGH HIS DEATH AND TRIUMPHANT RESURRECTION, JESUS demonstrated to the whole universe his VICTORY over the entire satanic kingdom! It is now our responsibility to demonstrate and administer the VICTORY Jesus Christ already paid for! To enforce, implement and execute the legal document of the GOSPEL of the KINGDOM! We need to understand that a triumph is not winning a victory it's the celebration of a victory that has already been won! The army that wins, is the one that advances! No army ever won a war on the defense; armies that win battles, advance and confront the enemy! The end times ARMY of God is the only army on the earth that has already won before we start to fight! *Colossians 2:14-15 KJV 'Blotting out the handwriting of ordinances that was against us, which was contrary to us, and took it out of the way, nailing it to his cross; And having spoiled principalities and powers, he made a shew of them openly, triumphing over them in it.* The Greek word for spoiled here is 'apekduomai,' which literally means to despoil, disarm, and stripped' So here we learn from this verse; *'Satan has been utterly destroyed, exposed, disarmed, spoiled and stripped of his power and Jesus Christ has left the enemy with no feet!' Matthew 16:18-19 NKJV 'And I also say to you that you are Peter, and on this rock, I will build My church, and the gates of Hades shall not prevail against it. And I will give you the keys of the kingdom of heaven, and whatever you bind on earth, will be bound in heaven, and whatever you loose on earth will be loosed in heaven"* JESUS speaks of his Church and sees his Church building and battling! We must have the mentality of building the Church and battling the forces of darkness! There is no building without battling! The Church should never be worried about how 'Satan will strike next, but Satan should be worried about where the Church will strike next! Much of the Body of Christ waits for the devil to hit, but we should hit him first! *Aggressive Spiritual Warriors is what God wants his Church to be! Hit evil when it is little and smack wickedness hard; do not wait for it to become a giant!*

AGGRESSIVE, VIOLENT SCRIPTURES THAT CONFRONT THE KINGDOM OF DARKNESS

None of these scriptures below say to 'wait until the devil attacks' then you can respond to him; no we're ready and equipped. When the devil attacks, we're already prepared for it and a step ahead of him by the Holy Ghost! We pray in advance, fast in advance, operate in spiritual warfare in advance, release spiritual-power in advance, forgive others in advance, and give tithes in advance! We're DOERS of the WORD in advance; we close all doors to the satanic kingdom in advance! Never giving the enemy legal ground and place in our lives!

Luke 10:19 YLT 'lo, I give to you the authority to TREAD UPON serpents and scorpions, and on all the power of the enemy, and nothing by any means shall hurt you' Pateo is the Greek word for tread 'which literally means to advance by setting foot upon, to trample under-foot, to crush with the feet' 'from this scripture we learn *"Christ has given us authority, governmental rule and jurisdiction through power of attorney, to tread-upon, to advance by setting foot upon, and to crush with the feet 'evil spirits and all of their power' then shall nothing by any means hurt you!* **Mark 16:17 KJV 'these signs shall follow them that believe; In my name shall they cast out devils.** The first sign that should follow believers is not divine healing, not miracles, not speaking in tongues, not prophecy! All of that is important, but the first sign is 'Casting out demons' **Matthew 10:1 KJV And when he had called unto him his twelve disciples, he gave them power against unclean spirits, to cast them out, and to heal all manner of sickness and all manner of disease.** JESUS never called anyone to preach the gospel of the KINGDOM; without authorizing them to heal the sick and rip Satan's kingdom to shreds! **Luke 10:9 'And heal the sick that are therein, and say unto them, the kingdom of God has come nigh unto you.'** Unfortunately, 70-

80% of the Church has been trained by carnal leadership to ignore Satan, when the bible teaches the opposite! JESUS, James, Peter, and Paul warned us through the below scriptures! We are never commanded to ignore the enemy, but to know who he is, know how he works, and expose him! To CRUSH, BRUISE, and DESTROY his works like Jesus Christ did! It is when we live our lives oblivious and unaware to the works of Satan that we fall victim to him, because we never confronted him, exposed his lies, destroyed his influence, and conquered his demon-inspired diseases, evil harms, and demonic affliction! ***James 4:7 KJV 'Submit yourselves therefore to God. Resist the devil, and he will flee from you.'*** Here, James said 'resist' the devil, which I might add is a daily process, not just at Church with a holy pucker on your face trying to look spiritual! *No, it's a daily resisting, confronting, renouncing, and bringing his lies into captivity to the OBEDIENCE of the Christ!* ***2 Cor 10:3-5 'for though we walk in the flesh, we do not war according to the flesh, for the weapons of our warfare are not carnal but mighty through God to the pulling down of strongholds. Casting down*** *arguments and every high thing that exalts itself against the knowledge of God, bringing every thought into captivity to the obedience of Christ.'* The Bible warns us about Satan and what he does to people 'he steals, kills and destroys lives' Never be oblivious, unaware, and carnally caught off guard! *1 Peter 5:8 'Be sober, be vigilant; because your adversary the devil, as a roaring lion, walketh about, seeking whom he may devour'* Here, Peter calls the devil an adversary; that as a roaring lion, the keyword 'as' because he is not a lion, he's a fake lion with a fake roar and no teeth! Because the Christ busted them out when he spoiled principalities and powers and made a spectacle of him in his triumphant RESURRECTION for the whole spirit-world to see! Satisfying the supreme court of the universe when he made propitiation for the sins committed by the people of God, now we can understand '*1 John 2:2 And he is the propitiation for our sins: and not for ours only, but also for the sins of the whole world.* Below Paul warns us, to never give place to the devil. *Ephesians 4:26-27 KJV 'Be ye angry, and sin not: let not the sun go down upon your wrath:*

Neither give place to the devil' We are commanded to expose Satan, not ignore him, and allow him to operate against your family, your marriage, your finances, and your health unchallenged! *Ephesians 5:11 TLB 'Take no part in the worthless pleasures of evil and darkness, but instead, rebuke and expose them.'*

JESUS ASCENDED BACK TO HEAVEN AND LEFT AN ETERNALLY DEFEATED DEVIL BEHIND

Satan knows he is eternally whipped, but he does not want you to know it! He wants to keep you ignorant of it, he wants you to blame God for what he does! *Hebrews 2:14 KJV 'Inasmuch then as the children have partaken of flesh and blood, He Himself likewise shared in the same, that through death He might destroy him who had the power of death, that is, the devil.'* Katargeo is the Greek word for destroy, which literally means to render idle, unemployed, inactive, inoperative, to cause to cease, put an end to, do away with, annul, abolish! Here we learn from this scripture that *'JESUS has left the enemy's power null and void; he has left him eternally defeated, inoperative, done away with, abolished and has put an end to the influence of Satan's kingdom in the life of the believer'* **Hebrews 9:12 'Not with the blood of goats and calves, but with His own blood He entered the Most Holy Place once for all, having obtained eternal redemption.** If JESUS obtained an eternal redemption for us and he did, that means he eternally defeated and eliminated Satan's influence in our lives! Now we can ACT on that, powerfully activate, implement, and decree that over our lives! **Rom. 4:25 YLT "who was delivered up because of our offences and was raised up because of our being declared righteous"** That is, he was delivered up to death, he was delivered up to pay the penalty we owed justice and when the claims of Justice were satisfied, then we were justified with the Christ! Right there in the presence of all the hosts of darkness, JESUS conquered the prince of darkness! **Hebrews 2:14 TLB 'Since we, God's children, are human beings—made of flesh and blood—he became flesh and blood too by being born in human form; for only**

42

as a human being could he die and in dying break the power of the devil who had the power of death.' He broke his power; now this is what I want you to notice: this was an eternal VICTORY, Satan's power was eternally broken, eternally conquered, eternally defeated, eternally eradicated and now the New Creation walks in that legally! And simply reminds the devil of his eternal defeat at the Cross by the Christ! *'1 Peter 5:9 'Whom resist steadfast in the faith'* our battle has been fought and won, there is no battle for you to fight except the battle of faith! You are to fight the good fight of faith. What does that mean? You are to win all your victories with words! You are to learn the words of this wonderful book, the Bible, and you will conquer your enemy with words! That is the way JESUS healed them, with words. That is how the Father created the universe, with words! You conquer the adversary with words! Now you can understand *'Psalms 107:20 KJV "He sent his word, and healed them and delivered them, from there destruction"* It is not asking the Father to do it, or asking the Father to do something he already did! Or asking him in anxiety and worry to deal with the devil for us! No, he already dealt with the devil eternally; now we rise in power, authority, anointing, and our faith in action, and put the rotten devil in his place! Under our feet, where the Christ placed him! Remember, what happened in the old testament symbolically happens in the new testament in reality. ***Joshua 1:3 KJV 'Every place that the sole of your foot shall tread upon, that have I given unto you, as I said unto Moses'*** God needs your feet, to crush the enemy on the earth! ***Romans 16:19-20 NKJV 'For your obedience has become known to all. Therefore, I am glad on your behalf; but I want you to be wise in what is good, and simple concerning evil. And the God of peace will crush Satan under your feet shortly. The grace of our Lord Jesus Christ be with you. Amen.*** This is a powerful Greek word for crush "suntribo" literally means 'to break in pieces, to put Satan under foot and (as a conqueror) trample on him; to tear one's body and shatter one's strength. So here we learn from this verse *"Through OBEDIENCE, when we are wise and practical to expose and resist evil, God himself will break Satan in pieces, place him under `our feet; so, as conquerors, we will tear; trample and shatter his strength*

by the grace of the LORD JESUS!' but Satan who was already defeated holds his Master the Church; the body of Christ in bondage! The utterly defeated one is binding his own master! According to the New Testament, the Church is given power and authority over an already conquered devil. Can you afford to subject yourself to Satan's dominion any longer? NEVER! Arise from this bondage, Confess that you are a CONQUEROR now in the Christ! Never have a picture of devils coming after you and overtaking you! Always have a picture of devils fleeing from you because your submitted to God, you're ACTING on the WORD of God! And you have the HOLY book on your side! *Always think of Satan as an eternally, utterly defeated foe; one over whom JESUS and you, in JESUS' NAME, have entire dominion, authority, and VICTORY over!*
1 Corinthians 15:57 KJV 'But thanks be to God, which giveth us the victory through our Lord Jesus Christ' *Now your end time God-given mission is to walk in the VICTORY, JESUS already won and demonstrate just how miserably defeated Satan already is, do you believe it?*

SATAN IS
A LEGAL EXPERT

He knows the law and accuses the brethren day and night, see '**Revelation 12:10**' He uses any legal right we give him and any crack as legal ground to continue exerting authority over the believer, even if it's a small area of your life. The unclean spirits refer to us as "their house" that they will stubbornly refuse to release and leave. In Matthew Chapter 12, JESUS gives us insight into the kingdom of darkness, how they view us, and what they call us. *Matthew 12:43-45 'When the unclean spirit is gone out of a man, he walketh through dry places, seeking rest, and findeth none. Then he saith, I will return into my house from whence I came out; and when he is come, he findeth it empty, swept, and garnished. Then goeth he, and taketh with himself seven other spirits more wicked than himself, and they enter in and dwell there: and the last state of that man is worse than the first'* He knows he can stay when unconfessed sin, agreements, and spiritual ties to his kingdom have not been dealt with. That is all he has; sins, lies we believe, spiritual ties, and evil soul ties that are cracks or entryways from mistakes we made in the past out of ignorance! ***1 Peter 5:8 KJV 'Be sober, be vigilant; because your adversary the devil, as a roaring lion, walketh about, seeking whom he may devour.'*** Here the Greek word for adversary is 'antidikos' which literally means *'An opponent in a suit of law'*

He's like a prosecutor, an accuser and a nitpicking, critical, faultfinding devil. I believe Satan knows the law better than most of the Church and he uses it against people when we are ignorant of his devices and what he is doing to the people of God. Most people in the Church blame God when something goes wrong! And believe that all the bad that happens in the world is God's fault. That is not biblical; JESUS made it clear when he said in ***'John 10:10, the enemy came to Steal, kill, and destroy, but I am come that they might have life and have it more abundantly'*** *The good news is we have heavens lawyer and counselor! We have the eternal comforter, we have an eternal helper! We have an advocate, the Mighty 3rd PERSON of the trinity, the Holy Spirit, and he has eternally acquitted, exonerated, and* *vindicated the people of God by the stripes, the BROKEN body, the excruciating death; resurrection, ascension; and exaltation of the Son of the living God Jesus Christ! Say Halleluiah!*

NOTES:

_____

_____

_____

_____

_____

_____

_____

_____

_____

_____

_____

_____

_____

_____

_____

_____

_____

_____

_____

Chapter 3

IT IS FINISHED

<u>AN IMAGE OF A COURTROOM IN YOUR SPIRITUAL MIND!</u>

I want to activate your imagination and help you understand what JESUS meant when he said in *John 19:30 KJV "It is finished"* The Greek word for finished is 'teleo' which literally means 'PAID' JESUS PAID the FULL PAYMENT for our sin! Your salvation is paid for, your divine health is paid for, your notable MIRACLE is paid for, your DELIVERANCE is paid for, your PROSPERITY is paid for, your PEACE, JOY, VICTORY and ETERNAL REDEMPTOIN is paid for! I want you to picture in your spiritual-mind a courtroom where we have a judge, "God the Father" *Psalms 7:11 says, 'God is a just judge,'* then we have a prosecutor in the Courtroom. "Satan the accuser of the brethren, an opponent in a suit of law or the adversary." *(1 Peter 5:8 Rev 12:10)* And you have a counselor, an advocate and a lawyer "the Holy Spirit" by your side helping you *(John 14:26,*

49

John 15:26, John 16:7) The prosecutor proudly says, your honor I have exhibit A 'proof of all the sin you've ever committed since you were 12 years old, "exhibit B he says "here's all the shame, guilt, negative emotions, hatred, self-hatred, pride, rebellion and unbelief, then the prosecutor says I have exhibit C "here's all the ungodly agreements he made with me, all the soul ties, generational curses from his family, the lies he believed and spiritual contracts that were made' And your opponent Satan then says, your honor according to ***Romans 6:23*** these sins are punishable by death; and he's asking for eternal death in outer darkness. The Judge quickly looks to your lawyer 'the Holy Spirit" for his rebuttal, he quickly says 'Your Honor may I approach the bench? He humbly says, your Honor the evidence presented by the prosecutor is true; however the defendant had a Substitute that took the penalty for the sins committed. Here's exhibit A "the BLOOD of the LAMB" Shed for the defendant, here's exhibit B, the Substitute was brutally murdered, shamed and hung naked on a Cross as payment for all sins committed by the defendant! The Holy Spirit, your advocate then says 'Here's exhibit C 'the divine substitute made propitiation for the sins and mistakes of the defendant having already satisfied the claims of justice and appeased the wrath of ALMIGHTY God. Here's Exhibit D "the Substitute was made sin, sickness and a curse *(2 Cor 5:21, Gal 3:13, Matthew 8:16-17, Isaiah 53:3-5)* "So that the defendant could be RIGHTEOUS, walk in divine health and live in the blessings of the KINGDOM of God" According to the evidence presented by the LAMB slain before the foundation of the world, your honor we request the defendant be exonerated, acquitted, vindicated and released by his faith in the FINISHED work of the divine SUBSTITUTE, the LORD Jesus Christ! The Judge boldly drops the gavel and Shouts *'My Son enter into the Joy of thy LORD, you are free, I am dropping the lawsuit and all charges against you! It is finished, you are free; you are free, you are free, It is finished!* Do you believe it son and daughter of God? Believing and acting upon this will change your life forever!

JESUS CHRIST WAS RAISED FROM THE DEAD, EXALTED TO THE RIGHT HAND OF GOD AND HE SAT DOWN

Colossians 3:1 KJV 'If ye then be risen with Christ, seek those things which are above, where Christ sitteth on the right hand of God.' 'Christ sat down at the right hand of God, there's a human JESUS of Nazareth seated at the right hand of ALMIGHTY God with scarred hands and feet interceding for us and representing us to the Father! As eternal High Priest in the order of Melchizedek ***'Ephesians 1:19-20 'and what the exceeding greatness of His power to us who are believing, according to the working of the power of His might, which He wrought in the Christ, having raised him out of the dead, and did set him at His right hand in the heavenly places'.*** We have the KING of KINGS, the Jewish MESSIAH, the LORD of GLORY, the glorious Christ seated on high, now we can understand ***'Philippians 2:9 'Therefore God also has highly exalted Him and given Him the name which is above every name'.*** He was raised, ascended, HIGHLY

EXALTED, lifted high and seated at the right hand of God. *'Acts 2:33 KJV 'Therefore being exalted to the right hand of God, and having received from the Father the promise of the Holy Spirit, He poured out this which you now see and hear.* People of God, did JESUS sit down? Yes, he did and because he sat down, that means the Father accepted what he did for us! And if the Father accepted, approved, and backs it by his throne! That means we have a perfect and flawless deliverance! In the mind of the Father, You are healed 'IT IS DONE!' JESUS knows that he bore your disease; how it must hurt him to hear you talk about you bearing them! When we learn to say, *'I am healed because he satisfied the supreme court of the universe'* that makes you free! We were healed when JESUS defeated Satan; stripped him of his authority; rose from the grave, ascended and exalted to the highest point in the universe and SAT DOWN at the right hand of God; Satisfying the claims of justice! *Hebrews 12:2 'Looking unto Jesus the author and finisher of our faith; who for the joy that was set before him endured the cross, despising the shame, and is set down at the right hand of the throne of God'.* Because JESUS sat down, we know and believe the Father accepted his sacrifice; approved his finished work, and backs it by his ETERNAL throne! And now we can count on what he did for us!

Hebrews 1:3 NKJV 'who being the brightness of His glory and the express image of His person, and upholding all things by the word of His power, when He had by Himself purged our sins, sat down at the right hand of the Majesty on high. The Greek word here for 'sat down' is 'kathizo' which literally means *'to confer a Kingdom on one'* when JESUS sat down, the Father conferred the KINGDOM of God on the Christ! And that means we can now manifest and display the RULE, REIGN, AUTHORITY, ANOINTING, FREEDOM, POWER, VICTORY, and TRANSFORMATION of HIS KINGDOM on the earth! Now we can understand.

Matthew 6:10 KJV 'Thy kingdom come. Thy will be done in Earth, as it is in heaven' We have no reason to live defeated lives because the KINGDOM of God has come and thy will be done!

NOTES:

_____
_____
_____
_____
_____
_____
_____
_____
_____
_____
_____
_____
_____
_____
_____
_____
_____
_____

EVANGELIST PETER VALENZUELA

Chapter **4**

WHAT IS DELIVERANCE?

DELIVERANCE IS THE DESTRUCTION OF THE KINGDOM OF DARKNESS BY THE KINGDOM OF GOD!

Col 1:13 Who hath delivered us from the power of darkness, and hath translated us into the kingdom of his dear Son.' The Greek word for translated is 'methistemi' which literally means 'to transfer, to remove from one place to another' Therefore, from this verse we learn; *The Christ delivered us from the power of darkness and has transferred us into his KINGDOM by removing us from and destroying Satan's kingdom.'*

CHRISTIANS CANNOT BE POSSESSED BY DEMONS!

However; evil spirits can get into your body causing sickness; or into your mind causing mental illness; in Matthew 15:22, the KJV uses the term 'demon possessed" let's read it *'**Matthew 15:22 "And behold, a woman of Canaan came from that region and cried out to Him, saying, "Have mercy on me, O Lord, Son of David! My daughter is severely demon-possessed'*** The greek word for demon possessed is 'daimonizomai' which literally means *'to be under the influence of a demon'* never does it mean 'possessed' by a demon! This has caused so many problems in understanding and accepting the Ministry of deliverance! However, we need to understand 'demonic influence or 'daimonizomai' in the life of the believer makes it difficult to obtain the perfect will of God. *Therefore, deliverance is the removal of the unclean spirits from the body and mind of the believer which is the Ministry of the Christ by the Holy Ghost in and through his end times ARMY and submitted-humble vessels of God.* JESUS bound the devil in order to establish his KINGDOM; we must align ourselves with the Christ through the end-times ministry of deliverance or else we have taken the devils side in this matter!

Matthew 12:28-30 "But if I cast out devils by the Spirit of God, then the kingdom of God is come unto you. Or else how can one enter into a strong man's house, and spoil his goods, except he first bind the strong man? and then he will spoil his house. He that is not with me is against me; and he that gathereth not with me scattereth abroad" From this scripture we understand the Christ is our deliverer by the Holy Ghost, which is how he establishes the KINGDOM of God. Here we see JESUS saying we must first bind the strongman; the strongman is Satan and Satan's house in verse 29 is the network of demons or the system of evil spirits within a person's soul. The word spoil in the Greek is 'diarpazo' which means to seize or plunder! The word 'goods' in the Greek is 'skeuos' which literally means *'an assistant in accomplishing an evil deed'* The strong man's goods or Satan's goods are his demons helping him 'accomplish evil deeds in the person's soul' which is what JESUS referred to as Satan's house in verse 29 '***Or how can one enter a strong man's house***' the word 'Can' in verse 29 is 'dunamai' which means *(to be able, to have power, to be strong and powerful)*

A literal concept of this scripture would say. *'When the KINGDOM of God comes unto us, Satan the strongman is bound, his goods or the network of evil-spirits will be spoiled; plundered and cast out of the soul destroying the house of the enemy, seeing the believer delivered and made whole by the Ministry of deliverance, which is how JESUS establishes the KINGDOM of God in their lives! If we are not on the same page with the Christ in the ministry of deliverance; we are against him, and scattering abroad—not gathering!*

DELIVERANCE IS KNOWING WE ARE IN A SPIRITUAL WAR AND ACTIVATING YOUR SPIRITUAL EYES

In 2021 I was in my bedroom one morning getting ready for work and I heard the small still voice of the Holy Spirit come to me saying *'spiritual eyes'* So I asked the Holy Spirit what this meant and in that season of my life, I was fighting a battle I couldn't win because I was battling the enemy with carnal eyes, focused and seeing what was wrong, not seeing JESUS and focusing on what he had already did for me and what he had already did to Satan! It is very dangerous to have powerful and active enemies working against you and not even be aware of it! The enemies we face are not flesh and blood, but invisible spirit-beings, or persons without bodies! In Ephesians Chapter 6, the Holy Spirit gave the apostle Paul a revelation of how the satanic kingdom is strategically set up and what were up against. In order to win, you must know your enemy! Champion prize fighters would study their opponent for years before they would enter the ring! Likewise, God the Father wants his Church to know who the enemy is! If the bible warns us about this person, Satan, and acknowledges him as a foe, an adversary and an opponent, we need to consider that ACT accordingly and deal with this devil like Jesus Christ did. ***Ephesians 6:12 (TLB) "For we are not fighting against people made of flesh and blood, but against persons without bodies—the evil rulers of the unseen world, those mighty satanic beings and great evil princes of darkness who rule this world; and against huge numbers of wicked spirits in the spirit world"*** Deliverance is dealing with the unseen realm, things we cannot discern with our natural 5 senses! The bible speaks about things that 'eyes have not seen, nor ear heard '

1 Corinthians 2:9 KJV "But as it is written: "Eye has not seen, nor ear heard, Nor have entered into the heart of man, The things which God has prepared for those who love Him. 'The invisible and spiritual realms can only be understood through God's WORD! People and most of the Church believe that what we see with the natural eye, touch and feel are more real than the unseen; but we cannot rely on our 5 senses, if we do we are already defeated! Your natural senses will deceive you and lead you astray; they are temporary, unreliable and unpredictable! We need to boldly say; *'I am not going to limit myself to the 5 senses; but by FAITH or the 6th Sense I am going to open my heart and my mind to Gods WORD that speaks of the unseen-invisible realm that can only be known by a revelation of the Holy Ghost and the WORD of God!*

NEVER LET THE NATURAL REALM STORM, STEAL YOUR SPIRITUAL REALM VICTORY!

Your spiritual realm victory has already been won in the Christ! Spiritual warfare is implementing unseen spiritual weapons and principles like the WORD of God, the faith of God, the Shed BLOOD of the Christ! And dunamis Mighty power in the spiritual-realm to obtain victory in the natural realm.

2 Cor 4:18 KJV 'while we look not at the things which are seen, but at the things which are not seen: for the things which are seen are temporal; but the things which are not seen are eternal.' The Greek word for look is 'skopeo' which means *'to fix one's eyes upon'* 'So now we fix our spiritual eyes on JESUS!' God wants you to activate your spiritual-eyes! If all you see is the natural-realm circumstance, that will distract, discourage and derail your divine-assignment! But if we can rise above fleshly, carnal, lazy, comfortable living! And live according to the spiritual principles God has set in place; we will walk in VICTORY and OVERCOME every attack of the enemy! We know were in a spiritual war, so now we activate our spiritual eyes! And the spiritual weapons of our warfare! ***2 Corinthians 10:3-4 NKJV 'For though we walk in the flesh, we do not war according to the flesh. For the weapons of our warfare are not carnal***

but mighty in God for pulling down strongholds' End time soldiers of the ARMY of God do not entangle themselves with carnal, fleshly, worldly, distractions that offend and derail the believer, instead they walk in self-discipline and focus on the call on their lives! *2 Timothy 2:4 NKJV "No one engaged in warfare entangles himself with the affairs of this life, that he may please him who enlisted him as a soldier."*

IMAGINE WAKING UP TO FIND YOURSELF COMPLETELY SURROUNDED BY THE ENEMY!

The prophet Elisha knew every move Syria was making and gave the king of Israel all of the enemy's plans. The king of Syria decided to take Elisha as a prisoner and sent an army to the city where the prophet was staying. Elisha's servant Gehazi cried out to his master in a panic, saying, what shall we do? Elisha was seeing this circumstance with his spiritual eyes, wasn't worried, wasn't afraid and wasn't concerned! He boldly and confidently says in

2 Kings 6:16-17 "Do not fear, for those who are with us are more than those who are with them. And Elisha prayed, and said, Lord, I pray, 'OPEN HIS EYES THAT HE MAY SEE' Then the Lord opened the eyes of the young man, and he saw. And behold, the mountain was full of horses and chariots of fire all around Elisha" As the Syrians began to advance on the city, Elisha spoke to God again, asking him to, "Strike this people, I pray, with blindness." Chaos broke out in the Syrian ranks as the entire army suddenly went blind. NOW YOU'RE GOING TO DO THE SAME THING! The natural realm storm isn't going to move you, causing worry and anxiety, No! *You're going to activate your spiritual eyes, the gifts of the Holy Ghost, the POWER of God, the anointing on your life, manifest KINGDOM authority, the WORD of God and the NAME of Jesus Christ! And like what he did for Elisha, JEHOVAH is going strike these devils for you with awesome power and crush the satanic kingdom for you! Obliterating, annihilating and eradicating every devil coming against your life and the call of God on you!*

DELIVERANCE IS A JOURNEY AND A PROCESS!

When JEHOVAH brought the Jews out of Egypt did it take one day? Was it an overnight deliverance? No, it was a process that took 40 years to enter the promised land. Now deliverance is not a cure-all; just because you spoke a prayer of deliverance; everything's not going to be perfect the next day! Satan will set you up for failure and discouragement! We have to be submitted to God and his process of delivering us; however that looks for us individually! The quicker we are fully submitted to God and his WORD, the quicker we renew our mind and obtain divine FREEDOM! *James 4:7 'Submit yourselves therefore to God. Resist the devil, and he will flee from you.'* Hupotasso is the Greek Word for submit, which literally means 'to obey, and to be subjected to 'anthistemi is the greek word for resist which means to set one's self against, to withstand, to oppose, or stand against' So from this scripture we learn that. *We are to submit to God, and obey him in all areas of our lives, resist, oppose, stand against, renounce, hate and withstand the devil and all of his influence!*

Then he will retreat, flee and vanish from you!'

PAUL SPOKE ABOUT A CONTINUAL DELIVERANCE PROCESS!

2 Corinthians 1:10 NKJV 'Who delivered us from so great a death, and does deliver us; in whom we trust that He will still deliver us." We preach and teach a 100% complete total deliverance from the enemy's kingdom! No compromise, no turning-back, no shame in that, no pride, no people pleasing and concern about what they say! However long it takes; whatever it takes; we pursue the enemies of the Church; evict them and cast them out of our lives!

PRINCIPLES OF DELIVERANCE FROM THE OLD TESTAMENT

We are told that 'we are to learn from the mistakes of the people of God in the Old Testament' and what happened in the Old Testament was an example for us. *1 Corinthians 10:11 NKJV "Now all these things happened to them as examples, and they were written for our admonition, upon whom the ends of the ages have come."* Also, the Old Testament was a type of shadow of the good things to come! *Hebrews 10:1 says, ESV "The law [was only] a shadow of the good things to come instead of the true form of these realities."* And everything they went through was for us to learn from *Romans 15:4 KJV 'For whatsoever things were written aforetime were written for our learning."*

OLD TESTAMENT SCRIPTURES THAT POINT TO THE MINISTRY OF DELIVERANCE!

JEHOVAH told the Jews in the Old Testament it was a little by little process, one spiritual inch after another and what happened in the Old Testament symbolically; happens in the New Testament in reality! *Exodus 23:30-31 Little by little I will drive them out from before you, until you have increased, and you inherit the land' - And I will set your bounds from the Red Sea to the sea, Philistia, and from the desert to the River. For I will deliver the inhabitants of the land into your hand, and you shall drive them out before you.* The Hebrew word for increase is "parah" which literally means to bear fruit, as we destroy the enemy in our lives, you will begin to bear fruit that you never had before. Your life will be fruitful in helping others obtain deliverance as you possess your New Testament promise land! *Numbers 33:51-53 "Give the following instructions to the people of Israel: When you cross the Jordan River into the land of Canaan, you must drive out all the people living there. You must destroy all their carved and molten images and demolish all their pagan shrines. Take possession of the land and settle in it, because I have given it to you to occupy."* Here JEHOVAH commands the people of God saying, *You must drive out all the people living there.'* These are a type of evil spirits that we must DRIVE-OUT with all diligence, persistence and boldness!

He has given us the New Testament promise land of divine healing, deliverance, the baptism of the Holy Ghost and eternal salvation and now we need to possess it! ***Deuteronomy 2:25 KJV "Beginning today I will make people throughout the earth terrified because of you. When they hear reports about you, they will tremble with dread and fear"*** These unclean spirits will fear you, flee from you, and be destroyed by you, CRUSHED under your feet, because they heard reports about you and quake, shake and tremble when they hear the NAME of the Christ released from your mouth in manifested KINGDOM authority! Fear not disciple of Christ, the enemy is already defeated and is terrified of you! ***Deuteronomy 7:16-19 "Also you shall destroy all the peoples whom the LORD your God delivers over to you; your eye shall have no pity on them; nor shall you serve their gods, for that will be a snare to you. "If you should say in your heart, 'These nations are greater than I; how can I dispossess them?'— you shall not be afraid of them, but you shall remember well what the LORD your God did to Pharaoh and to all Egypt: the great*** *trials which your eyes saw, the signs and the wonders, the mighty hand and the outstretched arm, by which the LORD your God brought you out. So shall the LORD your God do to all the peoples of whom you are afraid."* Like this Old Testament principle in Deut 7:16-19, we need to destroy every devil causing spiritual problems in our lives! There's no passive bone in your body and no compromising thought in your mind! Never glorify Satan and speak of him as having a victory over you, like 'Verse 18 'but you shall remember what God did to Satan, the New Testament Pharaoh' *Deuteronomy 7:21-23 "You shall not be terrified of them; for the Lord your God, the great and awesome God, is among you. And the Lord your God will drive out those nations before you little by little; you will be unable to destroy them at once, lest the beasts of the field become too numerous for you. But the Lord your God will deliver them over to you, and will inflict defeat upon them until they are destroyed."* Here we see that it will be a little by little process; one spiritual inch after another!' never expect deliverance to be a quick fix

71

or a shortcut! ***Exodus 23:29 "I will not drive them out from before you in one year, lest the land become desolate and the beasts of the field become too numerous for you"*** Here we see it is never a onetime event or a Joel Osteen prayer that fixes everything! Like the Israelites, JEHOVAH has a little by little process for deliverance; why would it be comfortable and easy for us? *Remember it took years to get into bondage; we need to decide to give God all the time necessary until the process is finished and we obtain all of the Children's Bread JESUS paid a HIGH PRICE for us to receive!* ***Deuteronomy 9:3 "Therefore understand today that the Lord your God is He who goes over before you as a consuming fire. He will destroy them and bring them down before you; so you shall drive them out and destroy them quickly, as the Lord has said to you."*** Like he did in the Old Testament, JEHOVAH as a consuming fire has gone before us by the finished work of Christ and paid for our deliverance and like the Israelites we need to drive them out and destroy them quickly! ***Judges 3:1-2 NKJV "Now these are the nations which the Lord*** *left, that He might test Israel by them, that is, all who had not known any of the wars in Canaan (this was only so that the generations of the children of Israel might be taught to know war, at least those who had not formerly known it."* Here we see JEHOVAH left the enemy in the promise land to teach and train his people to know war! And how to war a good warfare. He's doing the same thing in our life; these are the end-times and God is raising up end-time warriors; that will be ready to take the fight to the devil and destroy him! In the Old Testament if the people of God failed to drive out the enemy; JEHOVAH would allow them to live with them; intermarry, lead them astray and vex them in the land wherein they dwelled!

Joshua 15:63 "As for the Jebusites, the inhabitants of Jerusalem, the children of Judah could not drive them out; but the Jebusites dwell with the children of Judah at Jerusalem to this day."

Judges 1:21 "The Benjamites, however, failed to drive out the Jebusites living

in Jerusalem. So to this day the Jebusites live there among the Benjamites'

And so it is in the New Testament, if you compromise and fail to drive out the evil spirits; they will live with you and become a part of your personality, manifesting anger, hatred, negative emotions, discouragement; passivity, fear, doubt and unbelief! They will lay dormant and eventually cause problems later in life in your relationships, your finances, and your ministry because you wanted to be comforted instead of driving out devils and destroying their evil network! Don't give up and never compromise your freedom! ***Numbers 33:55 "But if ye will not drive out the inhabitants of the land from before you; then it shall come to pass, that those which ye let remain of them shall be pricks in your eyes, and thorns in your sides, and shall vex you in the land wherein ye dwell."*** Like the Jews in the Old Testament 'If we fail to drive out the evil spirits that are hindering, derailing and influencing our lives now; they will cause spiritual problems later; steal, kill and destroy various areas of our lives when we least expect it; that's why it is imperative we destroy and cast them out now! Notice JEHOVAH told his people, **'But if ye will not drive out the inhabitants of the land from before you'** Which are a type of New Testament unclean spirits! If we compromise and passively ignore the enemy, they will be pricks in our eyes; and thorns in our side, like a divorce, a porn habit that comes back to destroy you, a meth, pill or cocaine addiction that you entertained and back slid. Maybe sexual sin because you were never healed in that area of your soul. 'Pricks in your eyes' could be financial hardship, poverty and lack because you never demolished and cast out the unclean spirits of witchcraft poverty and loss of prosperity! How about hatred, anger and rejection that is ruining your relationships because you never cleansed yourself in those areas and received divine healing! Once you can boldly make a decision to rid your life completely of these devils and determine in your heart, you're going to see this through, NO MATTER HOW LONG IT TAKES, 'the Holy Spirit' will give you the Children's Bread and bless your soul unimaginably and incredibly! And you will not suffer loss, hardships, storms, sickness, premature death or witchcraft derailment, later in life! Because you BOLDLY did the WORD of God; CRUSHED, and TRAMPLED the enemies of God under foot like the Christ commanded you too! ***Luke 10:19 YLT 'Lo I give to you authority to tread upon serpents and scorpions and on all the power of the enemy and nothing shall by any means shall hurt you.'*** JEHOVAH God doesn't automatically remove devils from our lives! 'He's waiting to see our faith in action, he's waiting to see OBEDIENCE, BOLDNESS, and HATRED for the satanic kingdom! ***Judges 2:2-3 'But you have not obeyed My voice. Why have you done this? Therefore I also said, 'I will not drive them out before you; but they shall be thorns in your side, and their gods shall be a snare to you.'*** And it's when we begin to destroy the enemy in our lives 'the THRONE of God releases the GRACE of God in the area of deliverance by the BROKEN BODY of the Christ! And God will begin to drive the devils out of our lives! If we approach this ministry carnally; in compromise and ignore the warnings, these devils are legally able to stay! ***Leviticus 26:7-9 'And ye shall chase your enemies, and they shall fall before you by the sword. And five of you shall chase an hundred, and an hundred of you shall put ten thousand*** *to flight: and your enemies shall fall before you by the sword. For I will have respect unto you, and make you fruitful, and multiply you, and establish my covenant with you"* Notice JEHOVAH charges his people here to chase their enemies; and so it is in the New Testament, we are chasing unclean spirits out of our lives and destroying them! The Hebrew word for chase is 'raw-daf' which literally means to run after with hostile intent! So, from this scripture, we learn that *'We are to run after our enemies with hostile intent to conquer and destroy them!'* The spiritual truth is, we are either running after the enemy with hostile intent to conquer them; or they're running after us with hostile intent! See verse 8 *'And your enemies shall fall before you by the sword'* this is a type of a spiritual sword which is the sword of the Spirit or the WORD of God! *Deuteronomy 7:2 'And when the Lord thy God shall deliver them before thee; thou shalt smite them, and utterly destroy them; thou shalt make no covenant with them, nor shew mercy unto them.'* Here we see God promised to deliver the enemies over to his people. In the New Testament God has delivered evil spirits into the hands of believers as we have AUTHORITY over them in the NAME of JESUS! He told them to destroy and conquer, and show them no mercy; we are to do the same thing in the spiritual-realm in the New Testament. ***2 Samuel 23:9-10 'And after him was Eleazar the son of Dodo the Ahohite, one of the three mighty men with David, when they defied the Philistines that were there gathered together to battle, and the men of Israel were gone away: He arose, and smote the Philistines until his hand was weary, and his hand clave unto the sword: and the Lord wrought a great victory that day; and the people returned after him only to spoil.*** Here we see Eleazar first arose; and so it is with us, we must also be ready to CONQUER the evil spirits! Secondly, he engaged them by smiting the philistines until his hand was weary! 'Notice his hand was 'weary' we also may get weary in the CONQUERING of our enemies, but then it says his ***'hand cleaved to the Sword'*** like Eleazar, we are cleaving to a spiritual sword; which is the WORD of God. The result was ***'the LORD wrought a great victory that day'*** and so it will be with you; if you determine to smite and strike at your enemies! ***Exodus 13:17–18 'And when Pharaoh released the people, God did not lead them the way of the land of the Philistines, though it was nearer, because God said, "Lest the people change their mind when they see war and return to Egypt." So God led the people around by the way of the desert to the [Red Sea], and the [Israelites] went up in battle array from the land of Egypt.*** And so it is in the KINGDOM of God, there are no quick fixes or easy short-cuts! God almighty will take you through the difficult-tight; long, hard way, filled with affliction, storms and adversity; in order to humble you and prepare you for battle! So, you won't change your mind about following him when things get tough! *Be encouraged disciple of the Christ, JEHOVAH is training you and will see you through this vigorous and important season of deliverance! And like the people of Israel eventually entered the promise land and possessed it, so will you!*

Leviticus 20:24 "and I say to you, Ye-- ye do possess their ground, and I-- I give it to you to possess it, a land

flowing with milk and honey; I [am] Jehovah your God, who hath separated you from the peoples' The word possess is strong's Hebrew word 'yaresh' which literally means to occupy by driving out previous tenants and possessing in their place; to seize; to expel without fail; to cast out, to destroy, to succeed' so from this scripture we learn *'JEHOVAH has given us a land to possess, and by driving out the unclean spirits, destroying and expelling them without fail, we will succeed, occupy and enter in the New Testament promise land JESUS paid for'*

DELIVERANCE TAKES A HUMBLE HEART!

Matthew 18:4 'Whosoever therefore shall humble himself as this little child, the same is greatest in the kingdom of heaven.' We come to God as little children and receive all the deliverance he has for us, never assuming the purging and pruning process was done when we repeated a Joel Osteen 10 second sinners prayer! NO; there is child-like faith that needs to be activated to receive the KINGDOM of God and deliverance! ***Psalms 9:12, KJV: When he maketh inquisition for blood, he remembereth them: he forgetteth not the cry of the humble.*** God literally gravitates toward the humble because the heart is usually broken and ready for divine FREEDOM! ***Isaiah 57:15 'For thus says the High and Lofty One Who inhabits eternity, whose name is Holy: "I dwell in the high and holy place, With him who has a contrite and humble spirit, To revive the spirit of the humble, And to revive the heart of the contrite ones.*** It is the humble ones that will be delivered and used powerfully to become deliverers! ***Isaiah 66:1-2 YLT 'Thus said Jehovah: The heavens [are] My throne, And the earth My footstool, Where [is] this -- the house that ye build for Me? And where [is] this -- the place -- My rest? And all these My hand hath made, And all these things are, An affirmation of Jehovah! And unto this one I look attentively, Unto the humble and bruised in spirit, And who is trembling at My word'*** You know deliverance is precious because it cost the Father his Sons shed BLOOD at the Cross! Pride blocks deliverance and says, 'I'm good, I don't need help, I don't have any spiritual problems.' Satan was kicked out of heaven because of pride; pride has a satanic origin! God opposes the proud but gives grace to the humble! When GARCE comes deliverance comes! ***1 Peter 5:5-7 'Likewise you younger people, submit yourselves to your elders. Yes, all of you be submissive to one another, and be clothed with humility, for "God resists the proud, But gives grace to the humble, Therefore humble yourselves under the mighty hand of God, that He may exalt you in due time, casting all your care upon Him, for He cares for you.'*** Humility is a foundational key for deliverance; we must humble-ourselves to meet the conditions for deliverance! We need to let dignity go and obtain the Children's bread, we can keep our dignity but lose our deliverance! Dignity can come later once we have humbly been blessed, made whole and delivered! ***'James 4:6 KJV' But he giveth more grace. Wherefore he saith, God resisteth the proud, but giveth grace unto the humble.*** In the Young's literal translation 'JEHOVAH says he teaches the humble his ways. ***Psalms 25:9 'He causeth the humble to tread in judgment, And teacheth the humble His way'***

YOUR DELIVERANCE MAY NOT BE THE WAY YOU WANT IT

DELIVERANCE IS ALWAYS UGLY BECAUSE SIN IS UGLY! JESUS may want to know why you want deliverance; is it just so you don't have to suffer anymore and live carnally, fleshly and lazy? Is it to get blessed and live a comfortable; quiet, faithless life? Or are you seeking freedom so you can gain experience and be trained by the Holy Ghost to EXPAND HIS KINGDOM? That's what he wants, trained and tested end-time warriors! Never pursue deliverance for relief and freedom only! We must want all the deliverance the Christ has for us, to become deliverers! And freely GIVE what we received! ***Matthew 10:7-8 'As you go preach, saying the Kingdom of heaven is at hand, heal the Sick, cleanse the lepers, raise the dead, cast out devils, freely you have received, freely give'***

OBTAINING DELIVERANCE WILL TAKE PERSISTENCE!

It will take pure, radical, and desperate OBEDIENCE! Prayer and fasting needs to be a lifestyle to OVERCOME devils! If you can't commit to that; I wouldn't recommend you seek deliverance! In Mark 9:29 JESUS said to the disciples that couldn't cast out a devil, **This kind can come out by nothing but prayer and fasting'** *Persistence, boldness, tenacity, humility, grace and faith, along with the LOVE of God is how we ERADICATE the enemy's kingdom! Without persistence, we will end up in passive compromise and the enemy will gain the advantage! Blind Bartimaeus, was persistent; tenacious and aggressive!*

Mark 10:47-52 KJV 'And when he heard that it was Jesus of Nazareth, he began to cry out and say, "Jesus, Son of David, have mercy on me!"

- *48 then many warned him to be quiet; but he cried out all the more, "Son of David, have mercy on me!"*

- *49 Jesus stood still and commanded him to be called. Then they called the blind man, saying to him, "Be of good cheer. Rise, He is calling you."*

- *50 And throwing aside his garment, he rose and came to Jesus.*

- *51 So Jesus answered and said to him, "What do you want Me to do for you? The blind man said to Him, "Rabboni, that I may receive my sight."*

- *52 then Jesus said to him, "Go your way; your faith has made you well." And immediately he received his sight and followed Jesus on the road.*

Blind Bartimaeus was desperate in pursuing the Christ for his deliverance from blindness. We see that upon hearing JESUS of Nazareth was walking by, he immediately cried out to JESUS. He didn't hesitate, he wasn't worried, he wasn't uncertain or undecided. Secondly, he knew JESUS was the 'Son of David" verse 47 ***"Jesus, Son of David, have mercy on me!"*** By calling JESUS the Son of David, essentially he was saying JESUS I know who you are, you are the promised Messiah of JEHOVAH and he was saying King David is your ancestor, and that means you can open my blind eyes! Blind Bartimaeus knew the WORD of God and because he knew the WORD; he knew the promises of God; and because he knew the promises of God, he knew the Christ and the Jewish Messiah JESUS of Nazareth! So, when he heard he was walking by, he would take advantage of the opportunity to obtain his miracle at all costs! His attitude was, I won't be denied! Blind Bartimaeus probably knew the below scriptures about the Messiah, which equipped him!

Isaiah 35:5 'Then the eyes of the blind shall be opened, and the ears of the deaf shall be unstopped.

Isaiah 42:7 'To open blind eyes, To bring out prisoners from the prison, Those who sit in darkness from the

prison house.

Psalms 146:8 'The LORD openeth the eyes of the blind:

Blind Bartimaeus heard these scriptures read in the Jewish Synagogue all of his life. He was told for years that Messiah was coming! And when JESUS the Christ had finally arrived; blind Bartimaeus knew it, ACTED upon it, told JESUS who he was, expected his eyes to be opened and declared to JESUS! 'You are the Son of David and I have been waiting for you all my life! Throwing his garment aside in verse 50 signifying he wouldn't be begging anymore; and in Mark 10:52 'JESUS declared to him *"Go your way; your faith has made you well." And immediately he received his sight and followed Jesus on the road'* Will you do the same? Do you know who JESUS is? Do you know the word in the area you need a Miracle in? If you answered yes and you will be persistent, aggressive, desperate and tenacious, like Bartimeaus, you will be delivered, healed and made whole, because you will not be denied! *Even when religious folks with a holy pucker on their face tell you to be quiet, like they did to Bartmeaus 'WE NEED TO CRY OUT ALL THE MORE!' 'Verse 48 'then many warned him to be quiet; but he cried out all the more, "Son of David, have mercy on me!"*

IGNORING SATAN WON'T MAKE HIM GO AWAY

We confront him, expose him and destroy his works! As we enforce the **VICTORY** Christ won at the Cross for us! We know what he's trying to do and were always a step ahead of him, by the Holy Ghost! Ignoring him is only allowing him to operate unchallenged. Studies say 50% of Christians don't believe in a literal devil and that's exactly what he wants! *'Ephesians 6:10-12 KJV "For we wrestle not against flesh and blood, but against principalities, against powers, against the rulers of the darkness of this world, against spiritual wickedness in high places."* The word darkness is the Greek word 'skotos' which literally means ignorance. So, we learn from this scripture, *'Satan is the prince of darkness; and his kingdom is empowered and thrives on ignorance!'* God said my people perish for lack of knowledge, Satan wants us ignorant so he can freely steal, kill and destroy! I was a baby Christian, completely ignorant to the spirit-realm and Satan; bound by witchcraft-poverty, rejection unbelief and fear! *But when I was trained by the Holy Ghost in warfare, when he called me and taught me I could OVERCOME by the BLOOD of the LAMB and the WORD of my testimony; my life began to change!*

<u>SATAN IS THE ENEMY OF YOUR SOUL</u>

He's a malevolent personality, who wishes to do evil to others, the bible discusses this person Satan 200 times. The devil does not want the truth; he doesn't even want the truth about him to be revealed. He's a hiding personality, always hiding behind something, he hates exposure about himself and what he does to people! He would rather have people blame God for all the wrong that happens. *John 10:10 KJV "the thief cometh not, but for to steal, and to kill, and to destroy: I am come that they might have life, and that they might have it*

more abundantly" The Greek word for steal is 'klepto' 'Satan is a klepto- maniac, which is someone that has a recurrent urge to steal.

2 Corinthians 11:14 "And no wonder, for Satan himself masquerades as an angel of light" Satan is constantly deceiving people, making himself appear good, when he is not! People think spiritism is good, people think having your palm read is fun, people think the Ouija board is harmless and the occult is entertaining. People think Halloween is harmless and that trick or treating is fun! People think Yoga is healthy and good for you, people think because it's a white witch, it's a good witch; and that praying to Mary is a blessing! But in Ephesians 4:27 Paul said, **'Neither give place to the devil'.** There is no honor to him; no praise to him and no fear of him! Not one place in the bible are we told to fear demons, or to run from the devil, we're not cowards anymore! We BOLDLY fight, and are triumphant VICTORS in the LORD JESUS! ***2 Corinthians 2:14 KJV 'Now thanks be unto God, which always causeth us to triumph in Christ'***

NEVER LET RELIGIOUS FOLKS TELL YOU DELIVERANCE GLORIFIES THE DEVIL!

We're destroying him, tearing him to pieces, exposing him, crushing him, bruising his kingdom; trampling under-foot and treading-upon evil spirits! He would have been better off leaving you alone! And now we're getting payback, back pay, recompense and restitution by destroying his kingdom by the KINGDOM of God! EXALTING, and MAGNIFYING Jesus Christ, Son of the living God *Ephesians 5:11 'And have no fellowship with the unfruitful works of darkness, but rather expose them.'*

DELIVERANCE WILL REQUIRE YOU TO HATE THE DEVIL

Most of us were taught about the LOVE of God which is wonderful, but we were never taught that JESUS said if we LOVE God, we should hate and despise the devil *Luke 16:13 'no servant can serve two masters, for either he will hate the one and love the other, or else*

he will hold to the one and despise the other, ye Cannot serve God and mammon.' The Greek word for hate is 'miseo' which literally means *'to despise, to pursue with hatred, to detest'* Like JESUS we hate Satan, along with his cohorts, we despise everything they represent and what they do to people! We hate what the enemy does to kids; families, marriages, lives, finances, and people's health! Also hating sin will keep you from becoming a carnal Christian.

Hebrews 1:9 "Thou hast loved righteousness, and hated iniquity; therefore God, even thy God, hath anointed thee with the oil of gladness above thy fellows.'

Psalms 97:10 Ye who love Jehovah, hate evil, He is keeping the souls of His saints, From the hand of the wicked he delivereth them.'

Psalms 31:6 'I hate those who cling to worthless idols, but in the LORD I trust.

God will not deliver you from your friends, we must

decree and shout to the spirit-world! 'Gods enemies are my enemies and 'I HAVE HATED THEM WITH PERFECT HATRED!' ***Psalms 139:21-22 KJV 'Do not I hate them, O Lord, that hate thee? and am not I grieved with those that rise up against thee? I hate them with perfect hatred: I count them mine enemies.*** The glorious gift of hate is a must in order to break free, disagree, disannul and break all spiritual ties to the enemies defeated kingdom! God instructs us to hate Satan; and all his evil spirits!

Romans 12:9 'Love must be sincere. Hate what is evil; cling to what is good'

Proverbs 8:13 'To fear the Lord is to hate evil; I hate pride and arrogance, evil behavior and perverse speech.'

Psalms 119:104 'I gain understanding from your precepts; therefore I hate every wrong path.'

Eccl. 3:8 Solomon said there is a time to love and a time to hate

DELIVERANCE IS BEING ABLE TO TELL SATAN NO!

In Matthew 4:8-9 'Satan offered JESUS all the kingdoms of the world and their glory! He tried offering JESUS a shortcut and a quick fix to avoid the Cross if he would bow down to him. That is the type of outrageous; prideful devil we are dealing with, that demanded JESUS the eternal Mighty Son of the living God, to bow down to him. ***Again, the devil took Him up on an exceedingly high mountain, and showed Him all the kingdoms of the world and their glory. And he said to Him, "All these things I will give You if You will fall down and worship me."*** What is Satan offering you? Compromise and doubt; a quick fix, maybe lying and cheating to gain wealth. Sexual sin and witchcraft control, carnality, laziness, fear, doubt, unbelief or pride? Like the Christ we need to be able to say, 'NO DEVIL!' in Matthew 4:4 JESUS said, ***'It is written'*** verse 7 JESUS said ***'It is written!'*** In verse 10 'JESUS response to Satan's offer was `***Go – Adversary-'for It is written!'*** When we can address Satan and his demons with the WORD of God like

94

Jesus Christ did and BOLDLY Say

- *It is written 'I am the New Creation'*

- *It is written 'I Can do all things through Christ who strengthens me!'*

- *It is written 'I OVERCAME by the BLOOD of the LAMB'*

- *It is written 'Greater is he that is in me, than he that is in the world'*

- *It is written 'I prosper and walk in divine health, even as my soul prospers'*

- *It is written 'I was healed by the stripes of the Christ'*

- *GO adversary for It is written; I am more than a CONQUEROR and you must obey me!*

Then we are on our way to walking in the freedom wrought by the Christ for his beautiful bride. A few years ago, Satan offered me $8000.00 in commission that I didn't earn. It was a mistake my sales organization had made! I could have easily kept the commission and not said a word about it; but then he would have had an entry way and a legal right to destroy my finances. Instead, I reported it to my team and paid every penny back. *When we*

ACT on the WORD through conviction and integrity and say no to the enemy; we are declaring he has no right and he must take his filthy claws off every area of our lives; in JESUS MIGHTY NAME!

DELIVERANCE IS KNOWING WHO YOU ARE IN THE CHRIST!

The demons don't have to leave 'if we don't know who we are!' They know if we have genuine authority; they somehow know us and if we have a genuine relationship with God through JESUS! They know if we have genuine prayer lives and if we are truly and sincerely submitted to God and his KINGDOM! If we want to operate in spiritual warfare, spiritual-power and crush Satan's kingdom, we want to avoid what happened to the Sons of Sceva' in '***ACTS 19:13-16 KJV 'The seven sons of Sceva, took it upon themselves to call the name of the Lord Jesus over those who had evil spirits, saying, "We exorcise you by the Jesus whom Paul preaches. And the evil spirit answered and said, "Jesus I know, and Paul I know; but who are*** *you?" Then the man in whom the evil spirit was leaped on them, overpowered them, and prevailed against them, so that they fled out of that house naked and wounded.'* Satan doesn't want you to know who you are and whose you are! JESUS knew who he was; devils knew who JESUS was, devils know who we are; so many times, we ourselves don't know who we are! When we discover we are a new species; when we discover we are citizens of the KINGDOM of God with divine enablement and authority delegated unto us from heavens GOVT! When we discover we are a holy nation; and the one who spoke a universe into being has given us divine wisdom; we will be absolute Masters over evil circumstances that would have destroyed us in the past! *1 Peter 2:10 "Once you had no identity as a people; now you are God's people. Once you received no mercy; now you have received God's mercy."* You're a CONQUEROR, VICTOR and an OVERCOMER, that's who God say's you are!

Rom 8:37 KJV 'Yet in all these things we are more than conquerors through Him who loved us.'

EVANGELIST PETER VALENZUELA

1 John 5:5 'Who is he that overcometh the world, but he that believeth that Jesus is the Son of God?

1 Cor 15:57 'But thanks be to God, which giveth us the victory through our Lord Jesus Christ.'

Joshua and Caleb saw their identity in JEHOVAH; the other 10 spies saw themselves as grasshoppers, so the enemy saw them that way! **Numbers 13:33 KJV 'There we saw the giants (the descendants of Anak came from the giants); and we were like grasshoppers in our own sight, and so we were in their sight.**" With a new identity comes a new confession, we boldly shout to the spirit-world who God says we are! **Romans 10:9 "that if you confess with your mouth the Lord Jesus and believe in your heart that God has raised Him from the dead, you shall be saved.**"That word confession in the Greek means *'saying the same thing'* It means saying what God say's, and agreeing with God! Sons and daughters of God should have a mighty confession, no matter what the circumstance is! We boldly confess to the world, what God says we are! **2 Cor 5:17 "Therefore,**

98

if anyone is in Christ, he is a New Creation! Old things have passed away; behold, all things are become new" That doesn't mean were church-going, defeated- sinners; part of a halleluiah club waiting to get into heaven! It means what it says, we are God's New Creation; a new race, with the life; grace, ability and faith of God. We have the divine nature of God now and we keep his WORD on our lips! *Hebrews 4:14 "Seeing then that we have a great High Priest who has passed through the heavens, Jesus the Son of God, let us hold fast "Our Confession!"* Your confession about who God says you are; will stop the devil in his tracks and will put him in his place! What confession are we supposed to hold fast too? Amid all evil adversity and demonic attack! You declare, what Gods says. *'Greater is he that is in me than he that is in the world!* You Shout *'I am more than conqueror through him who that loves me!* You shout with a holy shout *'I am complete in him which is the head of all principality and power!* You decree 'I was healed in the crucified one! And I was delivered and made whole in the resurrected one! You declare *'divine power has given me all things that pertain to LIFE and godliness'* you believe and say *'Surely goodness and mercy shall follow me all the days of my life!* You boldly shout '*All my sins were forgiven, and all diseases were healed!* You make a governmental decree and say *I was delivered from the power of darkness and translated into the KINGDOM of the Christ'* And because the Christ is the high priest of your confession; when you confess what he did; *'He will make it good in your life'* **Hebrews 3:1 "Therefore, holy brethren, partakers of the heavenly calling, consider the Apostle and High Priest of "Our Confession, Christ Jesus.**

NOTES:
_____
_____
_____
_____
_____
_____
_____
_____
_____
_____

Chapter 5

WHAT ARE THE BENEFITS AND MOTIVATION FOR DELIVERANCE?

WE ARE COMMISSIONED BY THE CHRIST FOR DELIVERANCE!

WE HAVE BEEN COMMISSIONED TO DO THIS! WALK IN VICTORY, HUMBLE-MINDEDNESS, CLARITY and PROSPERITY! Imagine how glorious our dispensation is, we get to see the KINGDOM of God crush and destroy the enemy's kingdom like never before! That's exciting; exhilarating and your life is changed because of it! JESUS mandated, mantled and commissioned his Church to cast out devils when he sent us to preach the KINGDOM of God! *Luke 9:1-2 KJV* *'Then he called his twelve disciples together, and gave them power and authority over all devils, and to cure diseases. And he sent them to preach the kingdom of God, and to heal the sick.* Jesus Christ never sent anyone to preach the gospel that he didn't authorize to cast out devils!

Matthew 10:1 "he gave them power against unclean spirits, to cast them out, and to heal all manner of sickness and all manner of disease."

WITH DELIVERANCE COMES SUPERNATURAL JOY!

When demons leave you; your first response is supernatural joy! *When you overcome the satanic kingdom, you will walk in joy!* Wonderful, magnificent joy is a fruit of deliverance! And I believe joy is our response because we have just witnessed JESUS and his KINGDOM eradicate Satan's kingdom and it is wonderful to see the bible come alive! It is incredible to know we have hope and Satan can't do those things anymore that he got away with for years, because we didn't know it was him! That is exactly why JESUS came, to expose Satan and manifest his KINGDOM, his victory and his successful obliteration of the kingdom of darkness! *And when we get to be a part of this; you will receive supernatural joy like the early Church and your heart will bubble up with joy, joy, joy, joy down in your heart!*

Luke 10:17 'Then the seventy returned with joy, saying, "Lord, even the demons are subject to us in Your name" You too will experience this JOY after you receive deliverance and help others receive deliverance! *Acts 8:5-8 'Then Philip went down to the city of Samaria and preached Christ to them. And the multitudes with one accord heeded the things spoken by Philip, hearing and seeing the miracles which he did. For unclean spirits, crying with a loud voice, came out of many who were possessed; and many who were paralyzed and lame were healed. And there was great JOY in that city.* It's the JOY of the LORD and his JOY is our STRENGTH! *Nehemiah 8:10 KJV 'Do not sorrow, for the joy of the Lord is your strength."*

GOD WILL RESPECT YOU AND MAKE YOU FRUITFUL WHEN YOU DESTROY HIS ENEMIES!

Leviticus 26:8-9 'And five of you shall chase an hundred, and an hundred of you shall put ten thousand to flight: and your enemies shall fall before you by the sword. For I will have respect unto you, and make you fruitful, and multiply you, and establish my covenant with you'. Imagine that, 'JEHOVAH has respect for those that make it a priority to destroy the enemies kingdom!' He respects those that take this ministry seriously, because his Son paid a HIGH PRICE for it. It takes courage, boldness, faith, action, and a risk to wage war on the satanic kingdom! And JEHOVAH respects that! People will think you're crazy, people will accuse you of seeing a demon behind every bush, people will write you off and say you've gone too far, people will say you've joined a cult, and Satan will throw everything he can at you, to discourage you from seeing this through by the Holy Ghost! Jezebel will also rear her ugly little head if you allow her too! We must be careful too never compromise with that devil, because she will strike when you least expect it, try to derail your ministry, your integrity and your calling, all because she didn't get her way! Also be watchful of an Ahab that will allow her to operate in the Church unchallenged to thwart the ministry of deliverance! Wherever that unclean spirit is at work, there's always an Ahab afraid to confront her! ***Revelation 2:20 'Nevertheless I have a few things against you, because you allow that woman Jezebel, who calls herself a prophetess, to teach and seduce My servants to commit sexual immorality and eat things sacrificed to idols.***

YOU'LL BE AN HONORABLE VESSEL OF GOD BY THE CLEANSING PROCESS

Now you will be powerful; mighty, sanctified and perfected for a good work when you cleanse yourself of all evil influence, casting out all devils; and walking in the fear of God! ***2 Tim 2:20-21 'But in a great house there are not only vessels of gold and silver, but also of wood and clay, some for honor and some for dishonor. Therefore if anyone cleanses himself from the latter, he will be a vessel for honor, sanctified and*** *useful for the Master, prepared for every good work'* Paul was saying we have to be pro-active; advance, attack and confront the enemy's kingdom! Like you take showers daily, we have to take spiritual showers daily! 'Cleansing ourselves from everything unclean and their influence on our mind, will and emotions! Then you will be a vessel for honor, sanctified and useful for the Master, prepared for every good work!

2 Corinthians 7:1 'Therefore, having these promises, beloved, let us cleanse ourselves from all filthiness of the flesh and spirit, perfecting holiness in the fear of God'. Here we learn we are to cleanse ourselves 'which is a type of self-deliverance' from all filthiness of the flesh and spirit which are evil spirits, because your Spirit is wall to wall Holy Ghost; as we submit to the cleansing process, we are perfecting holiness and increasing in the fear of God which will lead us to hate and overcome sin.'

JESUS HUMBLED HIMSELF UNTO DEATH FOR YOUR DELIVERANCE

Philippians 2:5-11 KJV

- *5- Let this mind be in you, which was also in Christ Jesus:*

- *6-Who, being in the form of God, thought it not robbery to be equal with God:*

- *7-But made himself of no reputation, and took upon him the form of a servant, and was made in the likeness of men:*

- *8-And being found in fashion as a man, he humbled himself, and became obedient unto death, even the death of the cross.*

- *9-Wherefore God also hath highly exalted him, and given him a name which is above every name:*

- *10-That at the name of Jesus every knee should bow, of things in heaven, and things in earth, and things under the earth;*

EVANGELIST PETER VALENZUELA

- ***11-And that every tongue should confess that Jesus Christ is Lord, to the glory of God the Father.***

Here JESUS humbled himself, emptied himself, becoming obedient unto death, for our salvation, deliverance, divine healing, mind-renewal, and our complete REDEMPTION from Satan's kingdom and its influence! JESUS came to the earth to destroy Satan's kingdom and his works! ***1 John 3:8 KJV 'For this purpose the Son of God was manifested, that He might destroy the works of the devil.*** The Greek word for destroy is the word Luo 'the word Luo' here literally means to release, so from this scripture we learn! *'He's releasing you from sickness, disease, fear, doubt, unbelief, worry, anxiety and poverty! He's releasing you from Satan's lies that have derailed you for years! And loosing you from all the influence of satanic evil.*

DELIVERANCE SUSTAINS YOU THROUGH DEMONIC STORMS!

In 2018 after I bought my family a home, in a dream I witnessed my wife murder someone. I was asking why she would have done that if we just bought a home. This dream would prepare me fore what happened in 2019-2020! My wife decided she didn't want to be married anymore and left me and my kids for another man. My heart was trampled and broken by her actions. I remember spending my evenings crying, heartbroken and begging God to bring her home. Little did I know God was using this tragedy to break me, strip me from pride, prune, purge and bring more deliverance in my life! I realized my relationship was idolatrous and unhealthy, because I thought my identity came from my marriage! Pressing into the KINGDOM in that treacherous season of my life allowed me to CONFRONT, EXPOSE and CRUSH devils of rejection, lust, insecurity, fear and every other devil that was laying dormant in my soul. *Receiving the Children's bread in that season of my life; helped me stand firm in the KINGDOM of God. It was also a special time in my life, because his presence was powerful and I was truly broken!* I realized Satan's onslaught on my marriage to discourage me from pursuing a Ministry of deliverance, BACKFIRED on him! I spent those 24 months getting payback while ministering at the

AZ deliverance center; annihilating Satan's kingdom! And growing as a Minister of the GOSPEL of the KINGDOM. I witnessed the greatest Miracles and operated in a powerful ANOINTING; because God says he is close to the broken hearted and that his grace is sufficient, and his Strength is made perfect when I was weak! *I was able to grow tremendously in that season, remain in Gods will and not backslide on heroin or alcohol.* **2 Corinthians 12:9 'And he said unto me, My grace is sufficient for thee: for my strength is made perfect in weakness. Most gladly therefore will I rather glory in my infirmities, that the power of Christ may rest upon me.'** Sadly I have witnessed many people back slide and end up back on drugs when Satan attacks them through storms, trials and affliction because the network of evil spirits in the soul was never ripped to shreds and dismantled, giving the enemy legal rights to steal, kill and destroy lives, marriages and destinies! Paul said he was delivered first then translated into the KINGDOM of God. We must never take deliverance for granted and assume we have arrived without expelling demons and destroying the enemies influence on our soul (mind, will, and emotions) ***Colossians 1:13 'Who hath delivered us from the power of darkness, and hath translated us into the kingdom of his dear Son.'***

<u>FROM POVERTY TO PROSPERITY THROUGH DELIVERANCE</u>

Deuteronomy 8:18 'And you shall remember the Lord your God, for it is He who gives you power to get wealth.' Imagine being healed, delivered and blessed in all areas of your life except your finances? No, he wants you to live in prosperity, which is a benefit of KINGDOM living! How do we crush poverty? we drive out demons of poverty, lack, greed, and want! Then we give extravagantly and generously! We have to understand people of God, giving 10% is for baby Christians! The New Testament doesn't specifically say we should give 10% because God expects us to give more! Paul said the new covenant is greater than the former, why should tithing be any different? I know a KINGDOM millionaire that said he gives 80% and lives off of 20%. This was a paradigm shift and changed my life forever! When I began to give strategically and aggressively by faith, I began to see miracles in this area! I heard another Pastor *say 'If God can get money through you, God will get money to you!'* I was determined to give boldly, radically, and strategically! And I can sincerely say that God has done exactly what he said he would do! ***Malachi 3:10 'Bring ye all the tithes into the storehouse, that there may be meat in mine house, and prove me now herewith, saith the Lord of hosts, if I will not open you the windows of heaven, and pour you out a blessing, that there shall not be room enough to receive it.*** The KING is responsible to supply every need of his people! *'**Philippians 4:19 'But my God shall supply all your need according to his riches in glory by Christ Jesus'*** The KINGDOM economy operates completely opposite than the world's financial system! The world says lie, cheat, steal, keep your money, hoard it, and greedily take care of yourself! The KING of the KINGDOM says give and bless others! We give to the local Church for the work of the ministry, to finance the KINGDOM of God!

KINGDOM financiers give not to get, but to be able to give again! **Luke 6:38 'Give and it shall be given to you pressed down, shaken together, running over'** the greatest investment, the greatest return, the greatest reward, the greatest fulfillment, the greatest purpose is giving to the work of the KINGDOM of God! And when you obey, supernatural provision will be released in your life! Peter gave JESUS his boat to preach the WORD of the KINGDOM! After Peter gave JESUS his boat to preach the WORD! JESUS immediately released supernatural provision in his life! **'Luke 5:3-6 "Then He got into one of the boats, which was Simon's, and asked him to put out a little from the land. And He sat down and taught the multitudes from the boat.** Peter's boat was used to preach the KINGDOM! **When He had stopped speaking, He said to Simon, "Launch out into the deep and let down your nets for a catch 'But Simon answered and said to Him, "Master, we have toiled all night and caught nothing; nevertheless at Your word I will let down the net." And when they had done this, they caught a great number of fish, and their net was**

EVANGELIST PETER VALENZUELA

breaking.' What will JESUS release in your life when you give him your boat (finances) to PREACH the WORD of the KINGDOM?

The bible says when the Jews were delivered from Egypt 'Moses told them to collect silver and gold from the Egyptians! ***Exodus 12:35 'The people of Israel had also done as Moses told them, for they had asked the Egyptians for silver and gold jewelry and for clothing. And the LORD had given the people favor in the sight of the Egyptians, so that they granted them what they requested. Thus they plundered the Egyptians.*** God in the New Testament wants to give his people favor in the Market place! Favor with your clients, favor with your boss, favor in your imagination to come up with supernatural solutions, ideas and extraordinary problem solving skills! *To be the most dynamic, smartest and shrewdest Co-workers in your organization! The greatest problem-solvers and the hardest workers, walking in favor! Why? To be a KINGDOM financier! Never do it for the love of money, only for the LOVE of the KING!*

Chapter 6

HOW UNCLEAN SPIRITS GAIN ACCESS INTO OUR LIVES

SLAVES TO WHOM WE OBEY

Notice the scripture below says 'whom' which is a person, either Satan or JESUS is whom we are enslaved to! ***Rom 6:16 Do you not know that to whom you present yourselves slaves to obey, you are that one's slaves whom you obey, whether of sin leading to death, or of obedience leading to righteousness?*** Devils gain access to our lives through ancestral sin, and our sin. The wages of Sin is death, and the satanic kingdom is the enforcer of this death sentence, when we repent we receive the gift God promised. ***Romans 6:23 'for the wages of Sin is death' but the gift of God is eternal life through Jesus Christ our Lord."***

BELIEVING SATAN'S LIES ARE ENTERING INTO A SPIRITUAL CONTRACT WITH HIM!

The rejection demon is a strongman devil that invites others in through all forms of witchcraft and the occult! Devils gain access through all forms of sexual sin, the eye gate and the ear gate! They come in through victimization; if you were ever abused, physically, verbally or sexually molested. They come in through sins we committed, and sins committed against us! Well, you say that's not fair, who ever said the devil was fair? He's a dirty devil and will use any tactic or legal entry that is given to him! He doesn't play by the rules! The demons use a three-step process. #1 they lie first, the foundation of being demonized are lies! When we agree with the lie and accept it as our own thought then #2 the demon will bring feelings to back up and confirm the lie, then the demon has a legal right now. #3 they affect our actions and our behavior destroying lives, families and ministries! Satan attacks our thoughts; his priority is the destruction of the thoughts of the people of God; if he can get the mind, he has the Soul.

2 Corinthians 4:4 'In whom the god of this world hath blinded the minds of them which believe not, lest the light of the glorious gospel of Christ, who is the image of God, should shine unto them.
The Greek word for mind is Noema, which literally means 'a mental perception, or a thought' He wants your thought's because then he has your attitude, your action, your destiny and what you speak! That's why the bible encourages us to renew our mind! *'Rom 12:1-2 'I beseech you therefore, brethren, by the mercies of God, that you present your bodies a living sacrifice, holy, acceptable to God, which is your reasonable service. And do not be conformed to this world, but be transformed by the renewing of your mind, that you may prove what is that good and acceptable and perfect will of God'.*

<u>SATAN'S METHODS HAVEN'T CHANGED IN THOUSANDS OF YEARS!</u>

Ephesians 6:11-12 'Finally, my brethren, be strong in the Lord, and in the power of his might. Put on the whole armour of God that ye may be able to stand against the wiles of the devil'. The Greek word for wiles is 'Methodeia' which literally means *'deceit, trickery; methods'* his methods haven't changed, he's trying to deceive you through lies! And trick you into not believing Gods word! Trick you into believing that the lie you have been believing for the past 20 years is the truth, trick you into living your life according to the 5 senses and that your life is never going to change! God had given Adam and Eve his WORD; Satan came to Eve in '***Genesis 3:1 'The serpent said to the woman, did God really say, you shall not eat of every tree of the garden?*** The way he asked that question was to plant doubt and cause her to be indecisive and double minded. His methods are the same today, that's what he does to you; he seeks to make every Christian double minded and question the integrity of God's WORD! The enemy and the father of lies says; 'did God really say he loves you? Did God really say he's with you? He says 'you can't serve God' 'You'll never be free; you'll never be healed, he says, my power is greater.

Paul knew how the enemy works, that's why he says in '**2 Corinthians 11:3 KJV 'But I fear, lest somehow, as the serpent deceived Eve by his craftiness, so your minds may be corrupted from the simplicity that is in Christ.'** Another entry point and legal right Satan uses is the occult, psychic mediums, horoscopes, magic, any and all sorcery or witchcraft. Dabbling in the occult brings serious spiritual ties to the satanic kingdom! Unforgiveness is also a legal right the enemy will use against us; JESUS declared in '**Matthew 6:14-15 'For if you forgive men their trespasses, your heavenly Father will also forgive you. But if you do not forgive men their trespasses, neither will your Father forgive your trespasses.'** All sexual sin, perversion, dead religions; doctrines of demons; generational curses, word curses, and self-inflicted word curses give Satan entryway!

NOTES:

Chapter 7

CAN A CHRISTIAN HAVE A DEMON?

SATAN'S #1 LIE TO DISCREDIT THE DELIVERANCE MINISTRY

SATAN'S # 1 LIE IS THAT CHRISTIANS CAN'T HAVE DEMONS! He fills them with pride and with the attitude that deliverance is only for the heathen unbelievers in Africa or India not American Christians! 'How could God allow this? Is what the enemy whispers! The opposite is the absolute biblical truth; deliverance is only for the child of God according to JESUS, only for those in a covenant relationship with the great Hebrew God JEHOVAH through the Shed BLOOD of his son Jesus Christ! *Matthew 15:26 NKJV 'But He answered and said, "It is not good to take the children's bread and throw it to the little dogs."* In fact, we should never cast demons out of unbelievers, because they are not in a position to resist the devil and maintain their freedom which leads devils to come back with seven other spirits more- wicked than themselves and the final condition of that person is worse than the first! ***Matthew 12:45 NKJV 'Then he goes and takes with him seven other spirits more wicked than himself, and they enter and dwell there; and the last state of that man is worse than the first'.*** Another lie the enemy will use is that darkness cannot dwell in a believer where the Holy Spirit dwells, but my question is can a Christian be addicted to pornography? Can a Christian be sick? Can a Christian cuss and deal with ungodly anger? The answer is yes they can, which means a Christian can be both indwelt by the Holy Ghost in their Spirit-Man and be under the influence of the satanic kingdom in their soul, (mind, will and emotions) which are different realms and are not the same! The apostle Paul declared that nothing good dwells in him. **'Romans 7:18 'For I know that nothing good dwells in me, that is, in my flesh. For I have the desire to do what is right, but not the ability to carry it out.'** In another verse Paul declared the Holy Ghost dwells in him, did Paul get it wrong? Was Paul mistaken when he said sin dwelled in him and the Holy Ghost dwelled in him? No, he was speaking about his soul and his spirit-man!

Romans 8:11 'But if the Spirit of Him who raised Jesus from the dead dwells in you, He who raised Christ from the dead will also give life to your mortal bodies through His Spirit who dwells in you. We are composed of three parts, you don't have a spirit, you are a spirit, and you have a soul and a body. Your soul is completely different from your spirit; your spirit-man is the real you, the New Creation, more than a CONQUEROR-OVERCOMER, where the Holy Ghost dwells and lives in you! ***'1 Thessalonians 5:23 'LSV And may the God of peace Himself sanctify you wholly, and may your whole spirit and soul and body be preserved, unblameably at the coming of our Lord Jesus Christ'*** Your soul on the other hand is Satan's playground, the mind, will and emotions where Satan continues to influence (demonization) and attack the body through demonic sicknesses and diseases until we completely renew our mind and become spiritually mature, spiritually promoted and the anointing increases crushing the enemies influence by the KINGDOM of God. ***Hebrews 4:12 NKJV 'For the word of God is living and powerful, and sharper than any two-***

edged sword, piercing even to the division of soul and spirit, and of joints and marrow, and is a discerner of the thoughts and intents of the heart.' The bible makes a clear distinction between the soul and spirit. The Christ lives in your spirit; now we can understand '*2 Timothy 4:22 'The Lord Jesus Christ be with thy spirit.'*

A BELIEVER CANNOT BE POSSESSED BY A DEMON!

A GENTILE WOMAN SHOWS GREAT FAITH IN THE CHRIST! '*Matthew Chapter 15:22 'And behold, a woman of Canaan came from that region and cried out to Him, saying, "Have mercy on me, O Lord, Son of David! My daughter is severely demon-possessed.* That's a bad translation in the King James version, the word for demon possessed is 'daimonizomai' which literally means 'to be under the influence of a demon! '*Never does it mean possessed or owned by a demon!'* And that is what Satan has used to discredit the deliverance ministry!

I've heard it a thousand times "A Christian cannot have demons or be possessed by a demon" that is 100% true they cannot! However, after careful review of the word 'daimonizomai' we must conclude that the bible doesn't say a Christian cannot be demonized, leading us to assume they can. The Apostle Paul in letters written about Christians to Timothy show how Satan influences or demonizes the people of God. You will never read anywhere in the Pauline Epistles "Christians can't have demons or be harassed, influenced or afflicted by demons!" *__2 Timothy 2:26 'and that they may come to their senses and escape the snare of the devil, having been taken captive by him to do his will.__* Here Paul exhorts Timothy about some Christians that had been taken captive by Satan, to do his evil will! If Paul wrote to believers saying 'give no place to the devil' that means believers can give place to the devil. *__Ephesians 4:27 'neither give place to the devil.'__* We are commanded to resist the devil, and he will flee from us, 'that means it's possible that some believers aren't resisting him, and he's not fleeing! Causing problems, diseases, poverty and derailing the people of God.

James 4:7 'Submit yourselves therefore to God, resist the devil and he will flee from you' Paul wrote to believers encouraging them to not eat from the table of demons, which means they were eating from the table of demons and drinking from the cup of devils, being infiltrated by unclean spirits! *1 Cor 10:21 'Ye cannot drink the cup of the Lord, and the cup of devils: ye cannot be partakers of the Lord's table, and of the table of devils.*

JESUS CHRIST CALLS DELIVERANCE THE CHILDRENS BREAD ONLY FOR THE CHILDREN OF GOD

Matthew 15:25-28 "Then she came and worshiped Him, saying, "Lord, help me! But He answered and said, It is not good to take the children's bread and throw it to the little dogs And she said, "Yes, Lord, yet even the little dogs eat the crumbs which fall from their masters' table. Then Jesus answered

and said to her, O woman, great is your faith! Let it be to you as you desire."And her daughter was healed from that very hour" The bible boldly declares deliverance is the Children's bread only for the Children of God, because only a son and daughter of God are able to resist the enemy and keep devils out, in covenant with ALMIGHTY God by the Christ! We should never minister deliverance to carnal Christians or unbelievers; that will not submit to the VIGOROUS process of sustaining deliverance, self-discipline and self-control in FULL complete surrender to the Christ! In 2012 after ministering deliverance to a heroin addict at a Miracle service in Mesa AZ, the POWER of God was displayed and this young man was gloriously healed from evil spirits! So, I followed up on him a few months later and his mother told me he had recently overdosed on heroin; and was dead. I was heartbroken, and the Holy Spirit taught me a valuable lesson; and whispered to me *'Never cast demons out of unbelievers'* In another case, a young man was powerfully delivered from evil spirits in 2020 at a discipleship program in Payson AZ, sadly police officers shot and killed him a year later, because as a lukewarm carnal Christian, he backslid into meth addiction and the demons came back 7 times worse! *Matthew 12:43-45 "When an unclean spirit goes out of a man, he goes through dry places, seeking rest, and finds none. Then he says, 'I will return to my house from which I came.' And when he comes, he finds it empty, swept, and put in order. Then he goes and takes with him seven other spirits more wicked than himself, and they enter and dwell there; and the last state of that man is worse than the first.* JESUS called deliverance the "Children's bread" bread refers to life and sustaining power! Bread signifies a necessity, we need natural bread, and we also need the spiritual bread of the KINGDOM; that JESUS died to provide us with. *Luke 14:15 'And when one of them that sat at meat with him heard these things, he said unto him, Blessed is he that shall eat bread in the kingdom'.*

A GREAT LESSON ON DELIVERANCE IN THE LIFE OF LAZARUS

John 11:43-44 KJV And when he thus had spoken, he cried with a loud voice, Lazarus, come forth. And he that was dead came forth, bound hand and foot with graveclothes: and his face was bound about with a napkin. Jesus saith unto them, Loose him, and let him go. Lazarus death is a picture of salvation; when he was raised from the dead; he was still wrapped in his grave clothes and needed to be unbound! JESUS turned to the Church and said it was not his job to unwrap Lazarus! It was the Church's job to unwrap him. Often, we think after salvation; the grave clothes will automatically fall off! And that we do not need anyone to help us; but we need to be unwrapped by the LOVE and fellowship of the body of Christ in order to become the 'New Creation' The relationship between the believer receiving deliverance and the Church will determine the level of freedom and authority they walk in! *God ALMIGHTY has designed the local Church to be a safe haven for the disciple to obtain deliverance, sustain deliverance, walk in dominion, operate in the gifts; purpose, fulfillment, VICTORY, FULLY equipped and fortified in the KINGDOM of God!*

HOW DEMONS COME OUT

We see some evidence of how demons come out of people in scripture! And we must appreciate how they were expelled in the ministry of JESUS and model our ministries according to his ministry and his ETERNAL WORD! *'**Mark 1:26 'And when the unclean spirit had convulsed him and cried out with a loud voice, he came out of him.'*** We see that devils were released from people through the mouth with a loud voice or scream. And yes, deliverance will get ugly, but Sin is ugly! ***Acts 8:7 For unclean spirits, crying with a loud voice, came out of many who were possessed; and many who were paralyzed and lame were healed.*** Our spirits leave our body when we take our last breath, so when unclean spirits leave; they release out with a breath!

Psalms 104:29 'Thou hidest thy face, they are troubled: thou takest away their breath, they die, and return to their dust.' The most common ways are yawns, coughs, sighs, burps, and vomiting. The enemy will always try to bring shame, pride and guilt when it comes to this and when it gets ugly. *'We must* *understand, all that matters is that you're obtaining freedom in the Christ! And the demons are leaving; don't worry about how they leave or what someone else may think about you! This is your life, your destiny, your faith and your Holy Calling!'*

WE COMMAND DEVILS BY THEIR FUNCTION

After Satan's evil network or system of evil spirits has been dismantled and ripped to shreds, through the biblical strategy taught in this book, we will command evil spirits to leave by name according to their function! ***Mark 9:25 'When Jesus saw that the people came running together, He rebuked the unclean spirit, saying to it, "Deaf and dumb spirit, I command you, come out of him and enter him no more!"*** This scripture reveals JESUS commanded demons according to their function saying ***"Deaf and dumb spirit, I command you, come out of him'*** If the divine Master JESUS, the MIGHTY Son of the living God cast out demons and addressed them according to their function and what evil they cause,

then we should do the same! If people are dealing
with fear, we need to break that yoke, and drive out
spirits of fear! Your command might sound like
this, *'evil spirits causing fear or spirits of fear
come out of him in JESUS' NAME!'* If someone
is dealing with sexual sin, perversion and porn
addiction we would call the demons out by their
function saying *'unclean spirits of perversion
and sexual sin causing porn addiction, come
out of him in JESUS' NAME!'* The more
strategic and specific you are, the more effective
your deliverance ministry will be! We do not need
to spend 2 hours interrogating and questioning
demons, trying to figure out there name! Be
practical, and considerate of the person's time that
you are helping! And figure out what sin needs to
be repented of, what entryways need to be
renounced, proceed to break the spiritual ties and
begin to drive out the evil spirits, addressed by what
problems they are causing! A person dealing with
alcoholism will need the minister to command
*'demons causing alcoholism' or 'evil spirits
causing addiction to alcohol come out of him
in JESUS NAME!*

NEVER PRAY OVER OR COUNSEL DEMONS!

JESUS said we must 'cast them out' **Mark 16:17 *'And these signs shall follow them that believe; In my name shall they cast out devils'*** JESUS cast the demons out, he was never worried about what people thought or worried about offending them! JESUS speaking to an evil spirit said in '**Mark 1:25 *'And Jesus rebuked him, saying, Hold thy peace, and come out of him.'*** Paul, when speaking to demons said the same thing! '***Acts 16:18 But Paul, being grieved, turned and said to the spirit, I command thee in the name of Jesus Christ to come out of her.'*** The only way demons leave a person's soul is by being cast out. Never get religious and try to burn demons by the fire of God or command warring angels to do it for you! *Never focus on carnal, tangible feelings or demonic manifestations! Just do what JESUS did and you will be successful and cause a lot of problems for the rotten devil.*

DON'T BE DISCOURAGED WHEN DEMONS RESIST YOUR COMMAND

Mark 5:8-9 'For he said unto him, Come out of the man, thou unclean spirit. And he asked him, What is thy name? And he answered, saying, My name is Legion: for we are many. Here we see a demon resisted JESUS command to come out of the demoniac of Gadara. In Verse 8, JESUS commanded the demon to come out of him, in verse 9, JESUS was forced to expose the demon by asking its name, which was legion! A Roman legion in JESUS' day was 4800 men, this man had a system or a network of evil spirits in his soul' JESUS eventually drove them out into the pigs. If the demons didn't come out right away and resist the Son of God, you know they are going to resist his disciples! *'Stay persistent, continue to make commands like JESUS did, as we annihilate the satanic kingdom in the soul through repentance, renunciation, and activating manifest KINGDOM authority! Like legion, the devils will be UTTERLY destroyed and driven out whether it's 200, 500, or a legion!*

Chapter 8

LOVE IS THE FOUNDATION FOR DELIVERANCE

<u>JESUS BROUGHT A NEW KIND OF LOVE</u>

In my dream that I discussed previously, God showed me a mystery of the KINGDOM of God, LOVE is the greatest weapon against the satanic kingdom, and the glorious, UNCONDITIONAL DIVINE LOVE of God will literally DISMANTLE evil spirits! God's manifested LOVE is the foundation and force that evicts unclean spirits! The KINGDOM of God is built on LOVE! ***John 3:16 "For God so LOVED the world that He gave His only begotten Son, that whoever believes in Him should not perish but have everlasting life."*** Agapao is the Greek word for LOVE 'which literally means 'to love dearly, it is Gods divine UNCONDITIONAL wonderful, amazing out of this world; glorious life changing; game-changing LOVE in ACTION! This LOVE IS OURS! God LOVES you; He approaches us in LOVE!

135

The apostle John said perfect love casteth out fear! *1 John 4:17-18 "Herein is our love made perfect, that we may have boldness in the day of judgment: because as he is, so are we in this world. There is no fear in love; but perfect love casteth out fear: because fear hath torment. He that feareth is not made perfect in love.'* AGAPE LOVE CHANGED EVERYTHING! *John 21:15 "So when they had eaten breakfast, Jesus said to Simon Peter, "Simon, son of Jonah, do you love Me more than these?"* The word JESUS used in the Greek was agape; a LOVE which is of God, a self-sacrificing, divine, unconditional, supernatural LOVE! Not a friendly or romantic love, but of God's nature! The Greek word translated LOVE (agape) is not found in the Greek before the time of JESUS! Which means this new word agape was a divine revelation of the Christ. *AGAPE is not merely one of God's attributes; it is the essence of his nature. He can't help himself but to LOVE us! Zephaniah 3:17 "The LORD thy God in the midst of thee is mighty; he will save, he will rejoice over thee with joy; he will rest in his love, he will joy over thee with singing"* God has so many characteristics! He's awesome, Mighty, glorious, all POWERFUL, MAJESTIC, all knowing and omniscient, but most importantly 'HE IS LOVE' *1 John 4:8 Whoever does not love does not know God, because God is LOVE"* It's easier to trust and obey him because he is LOVE! This divine LOVE chose to save us before the foundation of the world, sent the Christ to the Cross and became sin for us! His LOVE heals us; patiently waits and pursues us until we decide to surrender! It never fails and never gives up on us! *This LOVE is not one of God's feelings or emotions; but it's the 2nd person of the Godhead, LOVE has a NAME, it's "JESUS!"* **Romans 8:37-39 KJV "Yet in all these things we are more than conquerors through Him who loved us. For I am persuaded that neither death nor life, nor angels nor principalities nor powers, nor things present nor things to come, nor height nor depth, nor any other created thing, shall be able to separate us from the love of God which is in Christ Jesus our Lord"** Human love is conditional, agape LOVE is unconditional, human love is changeable, agape LOVE is

EVANGELIST PETER VALENZUELA

unchangeable, human love is self-seeking; agape LOVE is self-sacrificing and unselfish!

THIS NEW KIND OF AGAPE LOVE IS A WEAPON!

Buried deep within every unbeliever is the need to be LOVED! Most of them have been abandoned rejected or hurt by a parent or family member! And just as carbon monoxide is deadly to our breath, so is LOVE to evil spirits! They cannot exist and work when surrounded by LOVE! *Agape LOVE forges a weapon that breaks down the hatred, anger and sin in the lives of others!* This is why JESUS taught us to LOVE our enemies! We are commanded by the LORD; to love those who seem least worthy of our love! LOVE is a powerful weapon in the hands of a skilled spiritual warrior! *'Matthew 5:43-44 "Ye have heard that it hath been said, Thou shalt love thy neighbour, and hate thine enemy. But I say unto you, LOVE your enemies, bless them that curse you, do good to them that hate you, and pray for them which despitefully use you, and persecute you. "* JESUS gave the New Creation a new commandment, if JESUS commanded it, there's no option here, we must obey; this would be proof that we follow the Christ! *'John 13:34-35 "A new command I give you: LOVE one another. As I have loved you, so you must love one another, by this everyone will know that you are my disciples, if you love one another!"*

DELIVERANCE IS NOT A CURE ALL!

Deliverance can never substitute for repentance, prayer, bible study and faithfulness to the LORD! However, what deliverance does nothing else can accomplish! Deliverance isn't the end; it's the beginning of your new life! Your freedom isn't only in deliverance; it's finding your identity in the Christ, It's the healing of the Soul; It's the renewal of the mind. It's acting on the WORD of God, which brings genuine transformation and mind renewal. It's taking up authority and filling your place in the local Church, by operating in the spiritual gifts of the Holy Spirit. It's submitting to valid authority God has placed over your life! And fellowship with the Church. ***2 Corinthians 3:17 KJV "Now the Lord is the Spirit; and where the Spirit of the Lord is, there is Freedom'*** *You can't do this alone, Satan wants you isolated; that's why God has designed the local body of Christ to protect you and help you stay free through the unconditional divine love of the Father released to you by the local Church of the living God.*

THE END TIMES FORCE OF GOD

Every branch of the US military has an elite force or special operations forces! The Army has Green Berets, and Rangers. The Navy has Navy Seals, and the Marines have RECON or amphibious reconnaissance! Well, the ARMY of God has an elite FORCE too! These special forces or elite warriors undergo difficult highly specialized and vigorous training to prepare them for battle. *God will strategically allow them to spend years in Satan's kingdom, addicted, heavily demonized and under witchcraft in preparation to turn the table on the devil. And to know how the enemy operates to bring others out.*

This elite force training surpasses training of ordinary soldiers! God uses both elite forces and ordinary soldiers in his army, some will focus on programs, numbers, tithers, personal ambition and notoriety, while God raises up special FORCES that will be on the front lines annihilating and eradicating Satan's kingdom and setting the captives free! And like JESUS they are the end times FORCE of JEHOVAH anointed by the Holy Spirit. '*Luke 4:18 The Spirit of the Lord is upon me, because he hath anointed me to preach the gospel to the poor; he hath sent me to heal the brokenhearted, to preach deliverance to the captives, and recovering of sight to the blind, to set at liberty them that are bruised'* The elite FORCE of God operates in deliverance! It is impossible to be an effective leader in the end time's Church without discerning and casting out devils! It is impossible to sincerely help people overcome Satan's evil tactics and attacks on the believer without deliverance! It is impossible to see lives truly and genuinely changed without deliverance! *You can be part of the carnal church living life according to your natural 5 senses never entering in the battle and never fulfilling the purposes of God or you can say yes to the Holy Spirit and be a part of Gods elite FORCE! And preach the KINGDOM of God!*

Luke 9:2 'And he sent them to preach the kingdom of God, and to heal the sick'

Luke 9:60 'Jesus said unto him, Let the dead bury their dead: but go thou and preach the kingdom of God'

Luke 16:16 'The law and the prophets were until John: since that time the kingdom of God is preached, and every man presseth into it'

God's FORCE will help people come out of Satan's clutches! This elite FORCE of God lives a lifestyle of fasting, revival, worship, and radical giving, submitted to God and his WORD! A lifestyle of hatred for Satan's kingdom, a lifestyle of seeking first the KINGDOM, doing what no one else does and seeing what no one else will see, a radical-annihilation of the satanic kingdom! **'Joel 2:11 'And Jehovah hath given forth His voice before His FORCE, For very great [is] His camp, For mighty [is] the doer of His WORD'.**

Chapter 9

THE 7 PRACTICAL STEPS OF DELIVERANCE!

THE 1ST STEP IS REPENTANCE

Repentance is the key that unlocks the door to the KINGDOM of God! ***Mark 1:15 "And saying, the time is fulfilled, and the kingdom of God is at hand: repent ye, and believe the gospel."*** The Greek word for repentance is 'metanoeo' which literally means to change your mind! JESUS said the KINGDOM of God is at hand; now we need to change the way we think and change our mind! We are Citizens of the KINGDOM of God and Jesus Christ is coming back to the earth real soon to establish his GOVT on the earth! We live the KINGDOM lifestyle of VICTORY through repentance and changing our mind!

<u>RELATIONSHIP NOT RELIGION</u>

It's important to know that people had spiritual ties under Satan's control before we come to Christ! ***John 8:34 "Jesus answered them, "Most assuredly, I say to you, whoever commits sin is a slave of sin"*** The only way to free ourselves from Satan's control is to submit to the authority and person of JESUS! Your authority in the KINGDOM of God is only as strong as your relationship with Christ.' ***John 8:36 KJV "If the Son, therefore, shall make you free, ye shall be free indeed"*** We can cast out devils all night, but deliverance will not be effective without a personal, intimate relationship with God through JESUS the Christ! ***Psalms 91:1-2 "He that dwelleth in the secret place of the most High shall abide under the shadow of the Almighty. I will say of the Lord, He is my refuge and my fortress: my God; in him will I trust."***

THE 2ND STEP IS BREAKING GENERATIONAL CURSES!

THE REALITY OF GENERATIONAL CURSES

We see the effect of sins and generational curses in operation in people in our daily lives! A curse is being empowered to fail; a blessing is being empowered to succeed! The bible explains the reality of generational curses! ***1 Peter 1:18-19 "For you know that it was not with perishable things such as silver or gold that you were redeemed from the empty way of life handed down to you from your ancestors, but with the precious blood of Christ, a lamb without blemish and without spot"*** But what God required for the sin and curses, God provided. The provision to break curses has already been paid for by the Christ of JEHOVAH' ***1 John 1:9 "If we confess our sins, he is faithful and just to forgive us our sins, and to cleanse us from all unrighteousness."*** JESUS the Son of God satisfied the claims of Justice; took the wrath of God that was due us, born of a virgin, and lived a PERFECT-SINLESS life! He created and established the Church of the living God, he was crucified; resurrected, ascended and exalted to the HIGHEST point in the universe! Now, because of what JESUS did; we can take back legal ground from Satan! When we break the curses, Satan loses authority and strongholds in our lives. '*Galatians 3:13 "Christ redeemed us from the curse of the law, by becoming a curse for us for it is written, "Cursed is everyone that is hung on a tree!"* We break curses by saying what the BLOOD of Jesus Christ has done for us! The Passover lamb of the Old Testament was a picture of Christ. *All that the Passover lamb revealed was fulfilled in the Christ! JESUS is the New Testament Lamb of God.* '*John 1:29 "Behold! The Lamb of God who takes away the sin of the world!* In the Old Testament, they used hyssop which is a small bushy plant to apply the lamb's blood on the doorpost! And when the destroyer saw the blood, he would pass over! *Exodus 12:22 'And you shall take a bunch of hyssop, dip it in the blood that is in the basin, and strike the lintel and the two doorposts with the blood that is in the basin. And none of you shall go out of the door of his house until morning.'* Now we apply the blood over the doorpost of our souls, by saying what the blood has done for us! Our mouth is the spiritual hyssop to apply the blood of Christ!

Psalms 107:2 'Let the redeemed of the LORD say so, whom he hath redeemed from the hand of the enemy.'

Rev 12:11 "And they overcame him by the blood of the Lamb, and by the word of their testimony; and they loved not their lives unto the death."

Some of the most frequent generational sin and curses that pass through the ancestral line are!

- *Abandonment*

- *Abuse, emotional, physical, mental,*

- *sexual Addictions, drugs, alcohol, meth, cocaine, nicotine*

- *Anger, rage, violence!*

- *Control, possessiveness, manipulation*

- *Fears – all kinds*

- *greed, lack, poverty*

- *Sickness, cancer, diabetes, all diseases*

- *Pride, Rebellion, bitterness*

- *Rejection, insecurity, self-hate & self-doubt, Low self-esteem; Inferiority*

- *Sexual sin and perversion*

- *Unbelief & doubt unto God*

- *Witchcraft, occult, Satanism*

ARE YOU READY TO BREAK CURSES?

DECREES ABOUT THE BLOOD OF THE LAMB BREAK CURSES 'I carried these in my car for over ten years, decreeing what the BLOOD of the LAMB had done for me! And repeatedly, continuously, forcefully, boldly shouting what the BLOOD was doing for me to the spirit world! And my life was literally forever changed! Begin to make these declarations over your life now and daily for the next 12 months! And you too will see exponential change and results in your life! See our website for the PDF under decrees. @ www.EXPANDMYKINGDOM.com

- *By the Blood of Jesus Christ I am the righteousness of God! 2 Cor 5:21*

- *By the shed BLOOD of Christ, I am justified! (Just as if I'd never sinned) Romans 5:9*

- *By the Shed Blood of Jesus Christ 'I am Forgiven and bought with a high price '1 Cor 6:19-20'*

- *By the shed BLOOD of Christ, I am washed from my sins – Revelation 1:5"*

- *By the Blood of Jesus Christ 'I am cleansed from all sin! – 1 John 1:7*

- *By the Blood of Jesus Christ "Satan your accusations are defeated and under the feet of Jesus Christ and his Warrior bride the Church!*

- *By the precious Blood of Jesus Christ; I am redeemed from all curses now! 1 Peter 1:19*

- *By the BLOOD of Jesus Christ, I was redeemed from the hand of the enemy! Psalms 107:2*

- *I overcame Satan by the BLOOD of the lamb and the WORD of my testimony! Rev 12:11*

- *Satan has no unsettled claims against me, ALL has been settled by the BLOOD! THANK YOU, JESUS!*

- *Now that all matters have been settled in the spirit-realm; every curse will retreat, cease and break in JESUS' NAME!*

ACTIVATION

ARE YOU READY TO BREAK CURSES?

REPEAT THE BELOW CURSE BREAKING PRAYERS, OUT LOUD AND BOLD!

- *In the NAME of Jesus Christ, I Confess all sin known and unknown!*

- *I confess and repent of all the Sin of my parents and ancestors!*

- *All sin is blotted out, wiped away and forgotten by God by the Shed BLOOD of the Christ!*

- *The shed blood of Jesus Christ stops all judgments and curses against me now!*

- *I am redeemed from the curse by the blood of Jesus!*

- *I am the seed of Abraham and I choose the blessing in JESUS' NAME*

- *I break and release myself from all generational curses and iniquities that were passed through the ancestral line*

- *I break and release myself from all curses of witchcraft, sorcery, divination and the occult in the name of JESUS!*

- *I break and release myself from curses of pride, rebellion, death and destruction in the name of JESUS!*

- *I break and rebuke all curses of sickness and infirmities in JESUS' NAME*

- *I break every curse of poverty, lack, greed, want and loss of prosperity in JESUS mighty NAME!*

- *I BREAK and loose myself from rejection curses, double mindedness; schizophrenia and mental illness in Jesus Mighty NAME!*

- *I break and release myself from all Jezebel and Ahab curses in the name of JESUS*

- *I break and release myself from all curses of perversion; sexual sin, soul-ties and body ties in JESUS Mighty NAME!*

- *I break and release myself from fornication; adultery; idolatry curses; accident proneness and premature death in JESUS Mighty NAME!*

- *I break and release myself from all word curses, self-inflicted curses*

- *I believe you're doing it now Father in JESUS Mighty NAME!*

Say thank you FATHER for breaking ALL the curses off my life in JESUS MIGHTY NAME!

THE 3ᴿᴰ STEP IS FORGIVENESS

We cannot expect God to do anything for us if we cannot forgive others! No matter what the circumstance was; many Christians do not realize how important it is to forgive, but for God; 'to hate a brother is the same as killing him!' ***1 John 3:15 KJV "Whosoever hateth his brother is a murderer: and ye know that no murderer hath eternal life abiding in him"*** Don't hide the negative feelings of hatred, unforgiveness, resentment, anger and bitterness that has been tormenting you for so many years! That's the barrier in your heart that has been stopping that long awaited blessing! ***Matthew 6:14-15 KJV "For if ye forgive men their trespasses, you're heavenly Father will also forgive you: But if ye forgive not men their trespasses, neither will your Father forgive your trespasses!"*** Forgiveness is not a feeling, but a choice! As you forgive others the Holy Spirit will soften and penetrate your heart and divine healing starts to flow. Every feeling of anger, hatred and resentment is an open door to the devil, these feelings once under Satan's control bring about depression, madness, suicide and every kind of disease! The bible doesn't say we cannot get angry, but God doesn't want it to last overnight, if you stay in un-forgiveness, we give place to the devil. ***Ephesians 4:26-27 "Be ye angry, and sin not: let not the sun go down upon your wrath: Neither give place to the devil."*** Now we confess our forgiveness before God, pronouncing the person's name; God is listening; Satan will see and hear your obedience and lose his authority over you! Ask the Holy Spirit to minister to you and reveal those places in your heart that are still bound by bitterness, hatred, self-hatred, unforgiveness, resentment and negative emotions toward others! It's your choice, don't wait any longer, forgiveness is serious KINGDOM business for KING JESUS; never compromise with it. If you won't forgive; you choose to give Satan a legal right and the advantage over, you, now we can understand

'2 Corinthians 2:10-11 KJV 'Now whom you forgive anything, I also forgive. For if indeed I have forgiven anything, I have forgiven that one for your sakes in the presence of Christ, lest Satan

should take advantage of us; for we are not ignorant of his devices' That Greek word for 'advantage' literally means *'to have more, or a greater part, to be superior'* we never want Satan to have more or a greater part of our soul because of unforgiveness! Forgiveness is a KINGDOM spiritual law that if not obeyed will invite the satanic kingdom in to torment you! Forgiving others is so important to God; that for there to be a perfect redemption, before JESUS could die, resurrect and redeem the Church, He needed to forgive the men that nailed him to the Cross! And the Jews that Crucified him! ***Luke 23:34 "Then Jesus said, "Father, forgive them, for they know not what they do!*** The Bible says that JESUS finished his work already and that he's seated at the right hand of God, He sat down AMEN! ***Hebrews 12:2 "Looking unto Jesus, the author and finisher of our faith, who for the joy that was set before Him endured the cross, despising the shame, and is set down at the right hand of the throne of God."*** But when you forgive others; JESUS stands up for you! How many of us want JESUS to stand for something we do for him? Here in the book of Acts we have the account of Stephen; who died the blessed death of a Martyr! ***Acts 7:55-59 "But he (Stephen) being full of the Holy Spirit, gazed into heaven and saw the glory of God, and Jesus STANDING (not seated) at the right hand of God and said, "Look! I see the heavens opened and the Son of Man standing at the right hand of God!" Then they cried out with a loud voice, stopped their ears, and ran at him with one accord; and they cast him out of the city and stoned him. And the witnesses laid down their clothes at the feet of a young man named Saul and they stoned Stephen as he was calling on God and saying, "Lord Jesus, receive my spirit." Then he knelt down and cried out with a loud voice, "Lord, do not charge them with this sin." And when he had said this, he fell asleep."***

The LORD JESUS stands up for us when we forgive others! If JESUS forgave his killers, we can forgive people no matter what was done!

Forgiving others is simply releasing them to God the Father to vindicate you and obtain justice for you, however he sees fit. But when we forgive, we are releasing the complete matter to Christ and Satan can no longer use that against us and cause problems in our lives!

THE PARABLE OF THE UNFORGIVING SERVANT IN MATTHEW 18

- *Verse 23 'Therefore the kingdom of heaven is like a certain king who wanted to settle accounts with his servants.*

- *Verse 24 'And when he had begun to settle accounts, one was brought to him who owed him ten thousand talents.*

- *Verse 27 'Then the master of that servant was moved with compassion, released him, and forgave him the debt.*

- *Verse 28 "But that servant went out and found one of his fellow servants who owed him a hundred denarii; and he laid hands on him and took him by the throat, saying, 'Pay me what you owe!'*

- *Verse 29 So his fellow servant fell down at his feet and begged him, saying, 'Have patience with me, and I will pay you all.'*

- *Verse 30 and he would not, but went and threw him into prison till he should pay the debt.*

- *Verse 34 'And his master was angry, and delivered him to the torturers until he should pay all that was due to him.*

- *Verse 35 "So My heavenly Father also will do to you if each of you, from his heart, does not forgive his brother his trespasses."*

When we don't forgive, JESUS will turn us over to the tormentors or torturers; See Verse 34 '**And his master was angry, and delivered him to the torturers until he should pay all that was due to him'** We may not have the ability to go and see that person, they may be dead, but we can confess our forgiveness before God, pronouncing that person's name! Satan will hear your obedience and again lose authority over you! Ask the Holy Spirit to minister to you and to reveal those places in your heart that are still bound by darkness. And to bring to light all the wounds that you have been covering and hiding for so many years in your attempt to forget them! It's your choice, don't wait any longer. If you don't forgive God cannot bless you! Are you ready to take action? Let's forgive those that have victimized us, harmed us, lied about us, molested us, rejected us, abandoned us, attacked us, talked about us and hurt us! *Ask the Holy Spirit to remind you of that incident or tragedy that happened when you were a child! Now quickly forgive them and release them! Now receive the Fathers forgiveness, and forgive yourselves! Do it now, as we do this Satan is losing authority over you!*

FORGIVENESS ACTIVATION REPEAT THIS DECLARATION!

- *In the MIGHTY NAME of JESUS!*

- *On the authority of God's HOLY WORD!*

- *I receive the Father's forgiveness!*

- *I forgive others! (Please verbalize specifics for genuine healing) ask God to heal those specific areas of your heart!*

- *I forgive myself (repent of all self-hatred, self-rejection and negative emotions toward self)*

- *Ask the Father to remove all the negative emotions towards that person!*

- *Say Father I ask you to heal this area of my heart!*

- *Say Holy Spirit I ask you to remove the negative emotions toward these people in JESUS' NAME!*

THE 4TH STEP IS RENOUNCING SATAN!

RENOUNCING Satan, is bringing everything out into the open that he has tried to keep hidden to use against you! The apostle Paul practiced renunciation! **2 Corinthians 4:1-2 KJV 'Therefore, since we have this ministry,** *as we have received mercy, we do not lose heart. But we have renounced the hidden things of shame.'* We cannot have any closed doors before the LORD when we are in his presence! Nothing can remain hidden from him; as deliverance is the result of a willing heart! When all doors have been closed to Satan the person will be totally delivered, as we minister, rely and depend on the Holy Spirit who will help close those doors forever; that is deliverance! To have people constantly manifesting, humiliating them and hurting their bodies is to do the work of the devil. Demons must leave when our authority and faith is put into action! If they don't, we missed something! It's never because of JESUS lack of power; he is LORD! *Job 1:1 "A man there hath been in the land of Uz -- Job his name -- and that man hath been perfect and upright both fearing God, and turning aside from evil.'* Turning aside from evil is renunciation! Many believers have not been taught that before they accepted the LORD, they had submitted their lives to a different lordship! They have never been led to renounce the authority and power that was given to the enemy, who may still maintain his position even if only partially oppressing the believer! To renounce means declaring that you want no more to do with this influence in your life, it is over! You want no more lies, and no more empty promises from Satan. Renunciation is an expression of repentance that believers never use and allows Colossians 1:13 to take place in our lives! ***"Who hath delivered us from the power of darkness, and hath translated us into the kingdom of his dear Son!"*** To renounce means to reject; to forbid; to abandon; to speak out, and to forsake; we are forsaking the kingdom of darkness. It also means to leave; we are leaving Satan's clutches and strongholds! This powerful word also means 'to refuse' we are refusing the devils empty promises now! When a person becomes a citizen of the United States of America; they are asked to renounce their home country for a new GOVT, the US govt. In the realm of the spirit, we are renouncing the kingdom of darkness for the KINGDOM of God! *Renunciation is giving the unclean spirits notice that you are on to them, and fully aware of what they are trying to do! Their time is up now and they must bow to the KINGDOM of God!*

- *You want no more lies!*

- *Their time is up!*

- *No more sin!*

- *No more bondage!*

- *No more death!*

- *No more failure!*

- *No more demon powers destroying our lives!*

<u>Renunciation does 3 things!</u>

1. *It identifies the lie and the power behind it!*
2. *It breaks the power of the strongholds over our minds, by giving notice to the evil spirits behind the lies that their lease has been terminated!*
3. *It gives us personal responsibility as an act of cooperation with the saving work of Jesus Christ!*

Frank Hammond said 'we can't get rid of a demonic tree unless you get rid of the root' renunciation is dealing with the demonic root; as we look for roots not just surface problems. It is good to know what Satan is trying to do, that's why Paul said 'we are not ignorant to the devils devices' As people renounce each vow they will undo each step that has led them to seal an agreement with the enemy!

THE HOLY SPIRIT WILL SHOW YOU WHAT THE ENEMY IS USING AGAINST YOU!

Job 36:8-9 'If they are bound in chains and caught up in a web of trouble, he shows them the reason. He shows them their sins of pride' When I was born again, I overcame heroin addiction, cocaine addiction and alcoholism; but the unclean spirits were attacking me in other areas of my life; like gluttony, mentally and in my emotions! So, God allowed demonic spiders to manifest and attack me, whenever I would eat too much! I had a dream in that season of my life; where God showed me, that I had unclean spiritual spiders in my stomach causing me to live in gluttony. I repented of gluttony, renounced gluttony demons, food idolatry, food obsession and broke their power off my life! I then began to cast out the demons of gluttony, food idolatry, food obsession and the lack of self-control. I learned that I should eat to live, not live to eat; and through careful and strategic warfare I overcame gluttony! Because the Holy Spirit tactically exposed the satanic kingdom! When I was initially delivered in 2011, I coughed up demons for about 4 hours and my eyes look like I was beaten with a baseball bat! Are you ready to renounce all satanic evil-entryways? *1 Peter 2:1 "Having put aside, then, all evil, and all guile, and hypocrisies, and envyings, and all evil speaking'* putting aside all evil is renunciation in action, renouncing the authority that was given to the satanic kingdom! *Colossians 3:5 "Put to death, then, your members that [are] upon the earth-- whoredom, uncleanness, passion, evil desire, and the covetousness, which is idolatry.* We have to put to death any and all legal right that was given to Satan, *James 1:21 "Wherefore having put aside all filthiness and superabundance of evil, in meekness be receiving the engrafted word, that is able to save your souls.'* Putting aside all filthiness of the flesh is renouncing Satan in all humility and when you do that, now you're in a position to receive the engrafted or planted WORD that saves you, delivers you and heals you! These scriptures are examples of renunciation! As you no longer compromise and passively allow the devil to operate unchallenged. Never let Satan bring shame, embarrassment, pride, passivity or compromise! At a recent outreach, this homeless woman had lupus, we led her in a few ministry steps; and as she was about to vomit devils out, she decided she wanted to hang on to the demons, and not fight! A few years after I was born again, the Holy Spirit showed me in a dream, that I was living under a witchcraft poverty curse due to idolatry in the ancestral line! After that revelation by the Holy Ghost, I was able to renounce the authority given to Satan; I broke the demon yoke and the agreements that were made with satanic idolatry! And forgave my family for entering into those spiritual ties. I then confronted the network of evil spirits in my soul; drove them out, little by little and broke the poverty curses! Literally, in a matter of 3 months, I received a $10k annualized raise! And my income has increased annually every year since that poverty curse was CRUSHED and DEMOLISHED by the Christ! Poverty, lack, greed and loss of prosperity is demonically ancestral and when you CRUSH these devils, renounce them! And begin to OBEDIENTLY give in this area, you will prosper even as your soul prospers! '*3 John 1:2 YLT 'beloved, concerning all things I desire thee to prosper, and to be in health, even as thy soul doth prosper'* Halleluiah for the ministry of the Holy Spirit that will reveal to you what the devil has on you! So you can renounce it, destroy them, forgive people and drive-out the devils in JESUS Mighty NAME! We must approach this as a strategic, tactical ARMY of God, with preparation and divine insight! If all we do is rebuke demons, all were doing is harassing the enemy; but if we undo what gave the demons authority and take back legal ground, the unclean spirits cannot return seven times worst! *Luke 11:24-26 When an unclean spirit comes out of a man, it passes through arid places seeking rest and does not find it. And when he comes, he finds it swept and put in order. Then it says, 'I will return to the house I left. Then he goes and takes with him seven other spirits more wicked than himself, and they enter and dwell there; and the last state of that man is worse than the first"* When people accept the LORD if they had previous debts or signed important financial agreements, those vows would still be enforced in the natural realm! Well in the spiritual arena,

before I was born again; I made allegiance to Satan through perversion, fear, poverty and death! I had so much unsafe sex before Christ that Satan led me to believe I had the aids virus, I literally believed that for years, summoning evil spirits of death into my soul, creating an infrastructure of evil spirits in my soul, 'the strongman being rejection, death, perversion and pride!' I needed to renounce the unclean spirits in order to be free! Even though I was born again and baptized in the Holy Spirit, they had legal rights and entry because of the pacts and vows I previously made before my encounter with the Christ! When we submit to a satanic priesthood, we have given Satan a legal right over our life, we must renounce all that was bound in the past! After accepting JESUS with all their hearts, people have to be ready to remove all that prevents the absolute work of the Holy Spirit! Be honest; and ask him what areas of your life are still in bondage! Don't let pride keep you from the freedom Christ has wrought for you! *When I think of demonic spiritual ties; I imagine demons carrying many ropes, these ropes bind us in different areas of our lives, when we discover what is causing the bondage and we renounce those ties; we cut off one of those ropes and then another and then another! Once all the demonic ropes are cut through renunciation, the demon will have nothing to stand on! Now we can boldly say, 'You have to leave in the NAME of JESUS! And the person will be FREE for the Glory of the Christ!*

DEALING WITH UNGODLY BELIEFS!

Disobeying God brings consequences that go beyond our imagination, if you decide to hide any sin from the Holy Spirit, or if you decide to believe any lies of the enemy rather than God's WORD, then the deliverance will be incomplete! Any thought that is contrary to God's WORD needs to be renounced and its power broken off your mind! You will need to fall out of agreement with it and make a bold decision and say no more lies! *No more compromise, no more procrastination, and no more passivity, even if the natural circumstance says the opposite; were going to believe God's WORD!* **2 Corinthians 10:3-5 "For though we walk in the flesh, we do not war according to the flesh. For the weapons of our warfare are not carnal but mighty in God for**

EVANGELIST PETER VALENZUELA

pulling down strongholds, casting down arguments and every high thing that exalts itself against the knowledge of God, bringing every thought into captivity to the obedience of Christ."

One day I asked the Holy Spirit what the weapons are, and this is what he told me!

- *The WORD of God, James 1:22, Psalm 107:20*

- *The SHED BLOOD of Christ, Rev 12:11, Col 1:13-14*

- *The POWER of the Holy Spirit ACTS 1:8, Phil 3:10*

- *The NAME of JESUS! Phil 2:9, Mark 16:17-18*

With these divine weapons; we crush, demolish, diminish and destroy the strongholds that exalt themselves above Gods holy WORD! The Greek word for 'war' in verse 3 is 'strateumai' which means to serve in a military campaign, or to lead soldiers to war, the greek word for 'pulling down' in verse 4 is 'kathairesis' which means 'demolition and destruction' the word 'Stronghold' here is a literal 'castle of evil thoughts that we've erected and

170

unclean ideas that we hang on too for safety' due to sins we committed or sins committed against us! In verse 5, the word 'casting down' is the Greek word 'kathaireo' which means 'to pull down, demolish with the use of force: to throw down, cast down, and to lower with violence' the word for imaginations in verse 5 is 'logismos' which means 'a decision' the word for captivity is 'aichmalotizo' means 'to lead away captive' (therefore a literal translation of this scripture would say) *'By the weapons of our warfare, we serve God in a military campaign, pulling down, throwing down, demolishing and destroying castles of evil thoughts, lies and unclean ideas that we set up in our mind to protect ourselves! As we activate the Mighty Weapons of our warfare 'the WORD of God, the BLOOD of Christ, the POWER of God and the NAME of JESUS' we cast down, throw down, pull down, demolish with the use of force and lower with tenacity and violence' every negative decisions we have been making all of our lives in our subconscious mind, destroying them and leading them away captive! As we replace them with the WORD of God in obedience to the Christ, as a DOER of the WORD of God instead of living our life according to a lie'*

We have to renounce the lies that have held us captive in the past, because what you believe will shape your destiny; that's why God wants our mind renewed! So many Christians are infected with ungodly beliefs or lies! *As we receive the Children's bread and deliverance takes place, we must reprogram our mind to be filled with the truth or we can give Satan a legal right and legal ground to return! As the Holy Spirit begins to sanctify our mind; our belief system begins to change from lies to the truth of God's WORD!* The goal is to be transformed into the image of the Christ walking in the Mind of Christ! While this goal may seem impossible to attain, we can decide to work with the Holy Spirit so that he can change us as rapidly as we can handle! Perhaps the day will come when we can say like the Apostle Paul!

1 Cor 2:16 "For who hath known the mind of the Lord, that he may instruct him? But we have the mind of Christ."

Phil 2:5 "Let this mind be in you, which was also in Christ Jesus:"

If God has promised us the mind of the Christ; let us pursue it boldly and aggressively with new thoughts; new expectations; new attitudes; new agreements; new decisions and a new belief system, as we become the New Creation!

Our spirits are redeemed when we are born again, the redemption of our mind is in process, and we can only believe the truth by having our minds renewed, otherwise, Satan has access to our minds because we believe his lies instead of the truth! **Ephesians 4:22-23 "That ye put off concerning the former conversation the old man, which is corrupt according to the deceitful lusts; And be renewed in the spirit of your mind."** Anything that doesn't line-up or agree with God's WORD is a lie from hell. Always remember that the rotten devil; Satan is a liar; JESUS said so! **John 8:44 "Ye are of your Father the devil, and the lusts of your Father ye will do. He was a murderer from the beginning, and abode not in the truth, because there is no truth in him. When he speaketh a lie, he speaketh of his own: for he is a liar, and the Father of it.'** Most of our ungodly beliefs result from childhood hurts or when somebody victimized us!

The lies of abandonment, rejection, and fear will powerfully affect our lives! They are lies that have been formed in us since childhood about ourselves, others, and God. They are formed from our experiences, hurts, traumas, and words people say to us. The ungodly beliefs can apply pressure and daily choke the abundant life that JESUS promised! The "perfect" ungodly belief is one that appears to be true based on natural facts of what happened to us in life yet is a lie according to God's WORD!

- *"I am unloved"*

- *"I will always be alone"*

- *"I am weird*

- *I am mentally ill"*

- *"God doesn't love me'*

- *"God doesn't care about me, because he allowed this to happen"*

- *"I will never prosper and be happy'*

- *"Something is wrong with me"*

Ungodly beliefs are:

- *Decisions*

- *Attitudes*

- *Agreements*

- *Confessions*

- *And expectations*

- *That does not agree with God and his WORD!*

Godly Beliefs are

- *Decisions*

- *Attitudes*

- *Agreements*

- *And expectations that agree with God!*

- *His Word*

- *His nature*

- *And his Character!*

Without mind renewal, you will never see God's perfect will for your life! According to Paul, we first offer our bodies as a living sacrifice, then we can be transformed by the renewing of our mind or in the Greek literal 'RENOVATED' in our mind! Then we are in a position for TRANSFORMATION, and the perfect will of God! That's why it is important for us to pursue mind renovation or mind renewal! Are you excited about renewing your mind; knowing the perfect will of God will manifest in your life once you do? ***Romans 12:1-2 'I beseech you therefore, brethren, by the mercies of God, that ye present your bodies a living sacrifice, holy, acceptable unto God, which is your reasonable service. And be not conformed to this world: but be ye transformed by the renewing of your mind, 'that ye may prove what is that good, and acceptable, and perfect will of God.*** You are promised the righteousness of God in Christ, supernatural peace from the PRINCE of PEACE, and unspeakable joy from knowing the divine Master! '***Romans 14:17 "For the Kingdom of God is not meat and drink, but righteousness, peace and Joy in the Holy Ghost***

HOW DO WE BREAK FREE FROM THE LIES WE'VE BELIEVED FOR SO MANY YEARS?

- *Identify the ungodly belief and expectation that does not agree with God's word!*

- *Ask the Holy Spirit to expose the lies underneath your fear, worry, anger, resentments, hurts, unbelief, doubts, and bitterness!*

- *Go for the root of the lies, and write out the ungodly beliefs!*

- *Start with ten so you're not overwhelmed!*

- *Confess and repent the sin of believing the lies instead of God's Word and living your life according to this lie!*

- *Forgive all that may have sinned against you or victimized you causing you to form the lie!*

- *Forgive yourself for believing a lie!*

- *Renounce the lie, and the authority you gave Satan by believing the lie.*

- *Now we break the power of these ungodly beliefs off your mind in JESUS NAME!*

NOW WRITE OUT THE GODLY BELIEF THAT AGREES WITH GOD'S WORD

- *Start with 10 so you're not overwhelmed!*

- *Pray the new Godly belief asking God to renew and quicken your mind according to the TRUTH!*

- *Confess and speak the new Godly beliefs and get them in your heart, mind, and your subconscious mind through disciplined meditation for the next 90 days!*

- *The Holy Ghost will now help you develop a new belief system, and he will show you more lies that need to be dealt with!*

- *This process and warfare could take up 6-12 months, even a few years!*

- *So don't be discouraged and NEVER give up!*

- *Be encouraged that as you follow JESUS and keep your eyes on him! Your mind is being powerfully RENEWED and you're being TRANSFORMED!*

Psalms 63:8 'My soul followeth hard after thee: thy right hand upholdeth me.'

Heb 12:2 "Looking unto Jesus —the author and finisher of our faith."

GOD FORGAVE OUR SINS! WHAT REMAINS ARE THE CONSEQUENCES OF THOSE SINS IN 3 AREAS!

The Physical, mental, and spiritual, as people renounce each vow, they will undo each step that has led them to seal an agreement with the enemy!

FOR PHYSICAL BONDAGE WE HAVE TO BE SPECIFIC FOR EACH SITUATION!

For Sexual Sin, heterosexual, homosexual, bi-sexual, adultery, fornication, lust, sexual abuse, rape, abortions, and victimization, your prayer might sound like this, *In Jesus' Name I renounce all sexual soul ties and body ties with (name of person) I renounce the Authority I gave Satan by submitting myself to that unclean spirit in Jesus' Name!* All decisions have to be confessed So, the enemy can know their time is up. Renunciation is issuing a spiritual eviction! Demons cannot read our minds, and they must be able to hear our decisions! In the case of an abortion 'Say 'I renounce all bondage to abortion' *I renounce all shame, guilt, resentment and condemnation, I ask forgiveness for having taken my child's life, I renounce the authority I gave to the spirit of death! Lord, I accept your forgiveness and I forgive myself in JESUS NAME!*

RENUNCIATION FOR THE SOUL, (MIND, WILL AND EMOTIONS)

- *Which include hate,*

- *resentment, pride, bitterness,*

- *rebellion, rejection, insecurity,*

- *fear, unforgiveness,*

- *Trauma, doubt, and unbelief*

For Specific bondage, you might say, in JESUS' NAME, I renounce all bondage of (hatred, bitterness, rejection) I have against (name of person) and I forgive him!

SPIRITUAL BONDAGE RENUNCIATION

All and any occult activity, Ouija boards, horoscopes, psychic hotlines, fortune tellers, tarot cards, palm readers, witchcraft, black magic, voodoo, and generational curses that were passed down! Any kind of contact with the occult produces very serious ties in the spirit realm, any consultation through horoscopes, or any method designed to predict the future leads to bondage and is an entryway for Satan to oppress and destroy! Everyone that has submitted to the counsel of a priest of the devil has yielded in authority to an unclean spirit. No matter what commitment or vow that was made, these pacts, vows and agreements have to be renounced and broken or they will remain! Your prayer might sound like this, *'In the name of Jesus Christ, I renounce all authority given to Satan when I (had my palm read, played with tarot cards, horoscopes, Ouija boards, witchcraft cleansing; in Mexico there called "Curandero") I renounce the authority I gave to the unclean spirits that operated in that situation and all the agreements and commitments that were made with Satan!*

ACTIVATING RENUNCIATION

- *Say in the NAME of JESUS, I renounce all evil*
- *I renounce ALL perversion impurity and sexual sin in the NAME of JESUS*

- *I renounce witchcraft, sorcery divination, occult involvement in the name of JESUS*

- *I renounce ungodly soul ties and immoral relationships in the name of JESUS*

- *I renounce hatred anger resentment revenge retaliation unforgiveness and bitterness in JESUS NAME!*

- *I renounce addiction to drugs alcohol or any legal or illegal substance that is bound me in the name of JESUS*

- *I renounce arrogance vanity Fear unbelief doubt selfishness in JESUS' NAME*

- *I renounce self-will, self-pity, self-rejection, self-hatred, and self-promotion in JESUS NAME!*

- *I renounce all ungodly thought patterns and beliefs systems, ungodly covenants, demonic vows that were made by myself or my ancestors in JESUS NAME!*

- *In JESUS NAME I renounce all evil works!*

- *In JESUS NAME I renounce all spiritual ties to Satan!*

- *In JESUS NAME I renounce all Covenants and agreements with Satan!*

- *In JESUS NAME I renounce all lies that brought bondage and fear!*

- *In JESUS NAME I renounce all negative inner vows, bitter root expectations, and all allegiance to Satan!*

- *In JESUS NAME I renounce all the authority given to Satan through all abused, verbally, sexually, or physically!*

- *In JESUS NAME I renounce all authority given to Satan through drug addiction!*

- *In JESUS NAME I renounce all authority given to Satan through physic powers, palm readers, tarot cards, spells, hexes and the Ouija board.*

- *In JESUS NAME I renounce covetousness and pride!*

- *In JESUS NAME I renounce voodoo curses, astrology, witchcraft and Psychic powers!*

- *In JESUS NAME I renounce suicide, depression, hopelessness and all evil powers!*

THE 5ᵀᴴ STEP IS THE HEALING OF THE SOUL

The soul encompasses the 'mind, will and emotions' God will heal us by divine power! And remove the scars in the soul from hurts, word curses, molestation, rape, sexual sin and family dysfunction! God has another level of healing of the Soul that some of us are not aware of! As a young man growing up in South Phoenix, I had powerful rejection demons attacking my soul. And after I was born-again, I was struggling in business because of self-rejection and the fear of rejection. My counselor at the time told me "I already have God's attention, his approval and his affection and my life began to change as I confessed that repeatedly for 12 months! I was wonderfully healed in my Soul through the CONFESSION of the WORD and the DUNAMIS power of the Holy Spirit! *The woman in **Mark chapter 5,** with the issue of blood for 12 years was healed by DUNAMIS power like you will be!*

- ***Verse 27 - When the woman heard about Jesus, she came up through the crowd behind Him and touched His cloak.***

- ***Verse 28 - For she kept saying, "If I only touch His clothes, I will be healed"***

- ***Verse 30 - And immediately Jesus having known in himself that out of him power had gone forth, having turned about in the multitude, said, 'Who did touch my garments?'***

- ***Verse 34 – Jesus says - 'Daughter, thy faith hath made thee whole; go in peace, and be whole of thy plague'***

The word for power in greek is 'dunamis' which means 'excellence of soul' JESUS first dealt with her Soul; then he said **'be whole of thy plague!'** Now we take hold of healing power; are you ready? Awesome and Mighty Holy Ghost POWER will heal your soul, remove the scars; bless your emotions, and heal your heart now, because you've already forgiven everyone, broken the generational curses, and renounced all evil. These scars that have hindered your relationships and ministry for years will be removed by the LOVE and healing power of the Holy Ghost! *Remember Gods WORD is just as powerful in your mouth as it is in God's mouth, because it's his WORD! And when you decree the WORD and the PROMISES of God you are activating heaven and the KINGDOM of God will shine light in your circumstance and change the trajectory of your life!* This was the pattern in my life, and I assure you God will do it in your life, because he is no respecter of persons! **Job 22:28 'And thou decreest a saying, And it is established to thee, And on thy ways hath light shone.'**

<u>DIVINE HEALING ACTIVATION</u>

- *I confess Jesus Christ has already paid for the healing of my soul according to Isaiah 53:3-5 and 'By his stripes I am healed' in JESUS NAME!*

- *Father, heal my soul and my Heart in JESUS MIGHTY NAME!*

- *Father glorify and magnify Jesus Christ.*

- *Say according to 1 Peter 2:24—My Soul is being healed now!*

- *Say 'the Miraculous power of God is flowing into my soul, healing me now; in JESUS NAME'*

- *Say 'the healing power of God is flowing into my Soul, body, and mind now in JESUS' NAME'*

- *I take hold of healing POWER now according to Isaiah 53:3-5, 1 Peter 2:24*

- *Holy Spirit healing fire is flowing into my soul now in JESUS' NAME, changing everything!*

- *Mighty healing power is flowing into my body now in JESUS NAME!*

- *Divine healing, soul saving, Miracle working Holy Ghost POWER is healing me now and I am recovering now in JESUS NAME according to Mark 16:17-18*

- *Holy Ghost, I ask you to remove all scars and hurts in my Soul that has caused repetitive-negative thoughts, feelings, and tormenting memories in JESUS mighty NAME!*

- *I have a right to the Children's bread because I'm a Child of the KING according to Matt 15:26*

- *Every unclean germ causing sickness in my body must leave my body now by the stripes of the Christ in JESUS' NAME!*

- *Jesus Christ bore all my sickness and curses on his body, therefore Satan has no right to put sickness on me in JESUS NAME!*

- *I crush and destroy every evil attack on my body now in JESUS MIGHTY NAME according to 1 John 3:8*

- *Christ makes me whole by his broken body, by his stripes, and by his WORD in JESUS NAME!*

- *On the authority of God's WORD, I command every mountain of sickness to get out of the way of my destiny in JESUS NAME according to Mark 11:23*

- *Father, I praise you and thank you that the Christ already paid for my divine health by his shed blood!*

- *Father, I have the receipt for my divine healing miracle; which is your HOLY WORD!*

- *I OVERCAME all sickness and disease by the BLOOD of the LAMB and the*

- *WORD of my testimony according to Rev 12:11*

- *Here's the power of a God flowing into my body destroying sickness, and healing me now in JESUS' NAME!*

- *Thank you, Father, I believe you're doing it now! I receive it now!*

- *Jesus Christ satisfied the Supreme Court of the universe! And Jesus Christ satisfied the claims of Justice for me!*

- *Jesus Christ satisfied the wrath of ALMIGHTY God at the Cross! And by his stripes I was healed!*

- *Father, I believe you did it and now I will ACT on your WORD*

- *Father I will do what I couldn't do before – for THY GLORY IN JESUS NAME!*

EVANGELIST PETER VALENZUELA

THE 6TH STEP IS THE CHURCH WILL BREAK SATAN'S POWER!

Romans 16:19-20 "For your obedience is come abroad unto all men. I am glad therefore on your behalf: but yet I would have you wise unto that which is good, and simple concerning evil. And the God of peace shall bruise Satan under your feet shortly. The grace of our Lord Jesus Christ be with you" Satan opposes the advancement of the KINGDOM of God and will do whatever it takes to distract, derail, and discourage us from destroying his kingdom. God glorifies his Son "Jesus Christ" when his bride destroys, stomps and breaks Satan's power! God is BRUISING Satan under your feet as you begin to ACT on the WORD of God referred to in this book! Are you happy? Are you ready to break Satan's power off your life? **Joshua 1-3 "Every place that the sole of your foot shall tread upon, that have I given unto you, as I said unto Moses."** You will now rise as the VICTORIOUS Church; bold as a lion, you renounced Satan, you forgave *everyone, we broke the curses off your life; you were healed in your soul and now we break the enemies power and destroy, diminish, conquer and annihilate the network of evil spirits, dismantling the strongman's house!* The US must know the strength of her enemy in order to attack accordingly! If we know who we're fighting against, we can know how to fight! ***Ephesians 6:10-12 "Finally, my brethren, be strong in the Lord and in the power of His might. Put on the whole armor of God - that you may be able to stand against the wiles of the devil. For we do not wrestle against flesh and blood, but against principalities, against powers, against the rulers of the darkness of this age, against spiritual hosts of wickedness in the heavenly places!*** Christ came to undo all his works and he has ordered us to do the same thing! The end times army of the LORD Jesus Christ is the only army on earth that has won the battle before they start to fight, so why give Satan any advantage? ***1 John 3:8 "For this purpose the Son of God was manifested, that He might destroy the works of the devil."*** If you have sincerely accepted the Christ in your heart; you have now been enlisted into the army of the LORD JESUS! *You're in a spiritual war and this is the fight of your life, JESUS has not called us to ask God to get the devil off of us! But he commanded us to do it, to drive him out and war a good warfare!*

1 Timothy 1:18 'This charge I commit to you, son Timothy, according to the prophecies previously made concerning you, that by them you may wage the good warfare.'

2 Timothy 2:4 "No one engaged in warfare entangles himself with the affairs of this life, that he may please him who enlisted him as a soldier"

JESUS has not called us to be passive and ignore Satan, but to engage him and OVERCOME! He gave us his authority, his NAME, his shed-blood, his WORD, his wisdom, and his POWER to finish what he started! **Mark 13:34 "For the Son of Man is as a man taking a far journey, (back to heaven) who left his house, (the Church) and gave authority to his servants, and to every man his work,** *and commanded the porter to watch."* Child of God you are called to engage the enemy! Deliverance is confronting and breaking the enemies power off our lives! *Mark 16:17-18 "And these signs shall follow them that believe; In my name shall they cast out devils; they shall speak with new tongues; They shall take up serpents; and if they drink any deadly thing, it shall not hurt them; they shall lay hands on the sick, and they shall recover."* You are MANDATED for such a time as this, to do the works of JESUS! *John 14:12 "Verily, verily, I say unto you, He that believeth on me, the works that I do shall he do also; and greater works than these shall he do; because I go unto my Father'* JESUS has "All authority over all evil spirits, all sin, all sickness, all bondage, all addiction, and all of the enemies lies! And he has given us that same authority. '*Luke 10:19, "Behold I give unto you power (authority) to tread on serpents and scorpions and on ALL the power of the enemy and nothing shall any means hurt you."* One of the greatest promises we have concerning protection is that

'Nothing shall by any means hurt us.' The Church is the greatest spiritual military power on earth and Jesus Christ has given us the keys of the KINGDOM to bind, and loose! ***Matthew 16:18-19 "on this rock I will build My church, and the gates of Hades shall not prevail against it. And I will give you the keys of the kingdom of heaven, and whatever you bind on earth will be bound in heaven, and whatever you loose on earth will be loosed in heaven.'*** We will now break the demonic yokes, spiritual ties, satanic covenants, evil pacts, satanic allegiance, unclean agreements that were made with the occult, witchcraft spells, negative inner vows and all authority we gave Satan through sin we committed and sin committed against us! *God Almighty has always wanted to take the people of Israel and the New Testament Church and break Satan's power and eradicate his kingdom!*

Jeremiah 51:20 "Thou art my battle axe and weapons of war: for with thee will I break in pieces the nations, and with thee will I destroy kingdoms;

Psalms 18:34 "He teacheth my hands to

war, so that a bow of steel is broken by mine arms;

Micah 4:13 "Arise, and thresh, O daughter of Zion, For thy horn I make iron, And thy hoofs I make brass, And thou hast beaten small many peoples, And I have devoted to Jehovah their gain, And their wealth to the Lord of the whole earth!

Psalms 2:9 "Thou dost rule them with a sceptre of iron, As a vessel of a potter Thou dost crush them.'

Psalms 68:20-21 "God Himself [is] to us a God for deliverances, And Jehovah Lord hath the outgoings of death. Only -- God doth smite The head of His enemies."

Zechariah 10:5 "And they have been as heroes, Treading in mire of out-places in battle, And they have fought, for Jehovah [is] with them, And have put to shame riders of horses."

Malachi 4:3 "And ye have trodden down the wicked, For they are ashes under the soles of your feet, In the day that I am appointing, Said Jehovah of Hosts."

Isaiah 58:6 "Is not this the fast that I have chosen, to loose the bands of wickedness, to undo the heavy burdens, and to let the oppressed go free, and that ye break every yoke?"

Exodus 15:6-7 'Thy right hand, O Jehovah, Is become honourable in power; Thy right hand, O Jehovah, Doth crush an enemy.

ACTIVATION

BREAKING SATAN'S POWER

Are you ready to break Satan's power off your life? Repeat this command; say 'In the NAME of Jesus Christ!

- *On the AUTHORITY of God's WORD! 'Listen to me Satan, take your filthy claws off my life!*

- *In Jesus MIGHTY-NAME I BREAK your power devil*

- *In JESUS Mighty NAME, I break every ungodly covenant and satanic pledge I ever made!*

- *I break and destroy every ungodly oath and agreements made by my ancestors In JESUS MIGHTY NAME!*

- *I break, and destroy all evil pacts and contracts made with idols, demons, and false religions in JESUS Mighty NAME!*

- *I break all covenants with death and hell made by my ancestors In JESUS Mighty NAME!*

- *I break all blood covenants made through any sacrifice that affected my life In JESUS Mighty NAME!*

- *I destroy any covenants made with false gods In JESUS Mighty NAME!*

- *I break all spiritual vows in JESUS Mighty NAME!*

- *I break the power of all agreements made with hell and darkness in JESUS Mighty NAME!*

- *Anger, hatred, unforgiveness, jealousy, envy, rebellion I break your power in JESUS' NAME!*

- *Rejection, self-rejection, fear of rejection, abandonment, insecurity, inferiority, timidity, I break your power in JESUS NAME!*

- *Passivity, depression, discouragement, hopelessness, suicide, worry, mental illness, I break your power in JESUS NAME!*

- *Schizophrenia, paranoia, confusion, mistrust, doubt, unbelief, doublemindedness 'I break your power in JESUS NAME!*

- *Demons causing mind racing, attacking my mind with lies, I break your power in JESUS NAME!*

- *Demons causing fear, pride, and deep-seated hurts, I break your power in JESUS' NAME!*

- *Demons that came in from mental, emotional, physical, verbal, and sexual abuse—in the NAME of JESUS I break your power!*

- *Gluttony, bad habits, nicotine, alcoholism, drug addiction, I break your power in JESUS mighty NAME!*

- *Lust, fornication, adultery, pornography, and sexual sin; I break your power in JESUS NAME!*

- *Witchcraft, Ouija board, palm reading, tarot cards, psychics, fortune teller, curses, hexes, spells, I break your power in JESUS NAME!*

- *Demons causing sickness, disease, pain, autoimmune diseases, hepatitis, diabetes, cancer; I break your power in JESUS NAME!*

- *You listen to me Satan, I break your chains off my life and my mind in the Mighty NAME of JESUS!*

THE 7TH STEP IS THE CHURCH WILL COMMAND EVIL SPIRITS TO GO

You cannot fool God and we cannot fool Satan; they both will know when we mean business! The key word is REPENTANCE! Stop playing around, stop playing church and get desperate! We will now command Satan to take his filthy hands off your life, because he has no legal right! It doesn't matter if there's 2, 3 10, 20, 5000 or a legion! When all ties are broken and commitments the person had with Satan are broken the enemy's activity in sickness, bondage and demonic influence will be terminated. There is no reason for an individual to continue in that miserable lifestyle. We must boldly declare that Satan has lost his authority over our lives! Then Jesus will say, did you hear that devil? 'They renounced you, you no longer have authority over their lives, and I'm taking them away from you!' *The devil is now forced to go, because he lost his authority and you can now enjoy the glorious freedom Christ came to offer!* JEHOVAH gave his people the promise land correct? But he required them to drive their enemies out of the land. Why would it be any easier for us to obtain the New Testament spiritual Promise land and all the promises of God! So it is in the New Testament, we must drive the devils out of our lives; the lives of our children and loved ones!

Deuteronomy 9:3 "Therefore understand today that the Lord your God is He who goes over before you as a consuming fire. He will destroy them and bring them down before you; so you shall drive them out and destroy them quickly, as the Lord has said to you'

Deuteronomy 33:27 "The eternal God is a hiding place, And underneath are the everlasting arms; And He drove out the enemy from you, And said, 'Destroy!'

Mark 16:17 "these signs will follow those who believe: In My name they will cast out demons;

Matthew 10:1 'And when he had called unto him his twelve disciples, he gave them power against unclean spirits, to cast them out, and to heal all manner of sickness and all manner of

disease.

Luke 4:18 "The Spirit of the Lord is upon me, because he hath anointed me to preach the gospel to the poor; he hath sent me to heal the brokenhearted, to preach deliverance to the captives, and recovering of sight to the blind, to set at liberty them that are bruised"

The Christ came to preach deliverance and you are the fulfillment of that! We might boldly say with authority *'Now in the NAME of JESUS; unclean spirits come out of him!* The Church can now boldly say "Now that all matters have been settled in the spirit-realm' you filthy, unclean spirits come out of him now! Aggressively-persistently, boldly commanding and demanding the evil spirits to leave the person, because they can't hide anymore! *A Christian without deliverance becomes distracted and backslidden, never living the life of an OVERCOMER, but when the Children's bread is obtained; we can now fulfill the call of God on our lives!*

Matthew 10:1 "And when he had called unto him his twelve disciples, he gave

them power against unclean spirits, to cast them out, and to heal all manner of sickness and all manner of disease.

Matthew 10:8 "_Heal the sick, cleanse the lepers, raise the dead, cast out devils: freely ye have received, freely give.

Leviticus 26:7-9 "And ye have pursued your enemies, and they have fallen before you by the sword; and five of you have pursued a hundred, and a hundred of you do pursue a myriad; and your enemies have fallen before you by the sword. And I have turned unto you, and have made you fruitful, and have multiplied you, and have established My covenant with you.'

ARE YOU READY TO RECEIVE THE GLORIOUS FREEDOM JESUS DIED TO PROVIDE US?

Let's humble ourselves under the mighty hand of God that he may exalt us in due time;

make this decree!

- *I declare this is Holy Ground*

- *Devil you know what I know!*

- *You are exposed*

- *POOR devil; I bind you in JESUS NAME!*

- *I rebuke every unclean spirit in JESUS NAME!*

- *In the NAME above all NAMES JESUS; I command you to take your filthy claws off my life now!*

- *You have to leave now; you have no option and no open doors!*

- *Father I thank you for deliverance now!*

- *Father you're doing it now; thank you JESUS!*

Read the list below in areas you're struggling in and boldly command the devils to GO!

SEE LIST OF UNCLEAN SPIRITS THAT MUST GO NOW!

EVIL SPIRITS OF REJECTION, RESENTMENT AND SELF HATRED

Spirits of rejection, Rejection spirits

Rejection by parents, Rejection by family

Rejection by kids, Rejection by spouse

Rejection by girls in elementary school

Rejection by boys in elementary school

Self-rejection, fear of rejection

Rejecting others before thy reject me; expecting to be rejected

Roots of bitterness, Resentment; bitterness and hatred

Hatred, self-hatred, Un-forgiveness

Soul-Hurts, deep seated pain, spirits of Hurts; heartache; and heartbreak

Spirits of disappointment, I lay the AX to the root of rejection

Prenatal rejection, parental rejection, Rejection and loneliness

Insecurity, Fear of rejection and self-rejection

Rebellion, self-hatred, Hatred toward parents

COME OUT IN JESUS NAME!

UNCLEAN SPIRITS OF LUST AND SEXUAL SIN

Evil spirits of sexual bondage

Spirits of Lust, spirits of fornication

Lust in the mind, Fantasy lust, Lust for woman

Lust for men, spirits of Incest

Sexual torment of the mind, Ungodly sexual soul ties

Ungodly sexual body ties, sexual imaginations

Demons that came in from molestation

Homosexual desire, lesbian spirits, bi-sexual spirits

Orgy spirits, oral sex spirits

Craving sex spirits, seduction curses

Sexual prey, Inherited Sexual sin curses

Occult seduction spirits, Illegitimate curses

Sexual deviance spirits, bestiality Spirits

Pornography spirits, adultery spirits

Lust of the eyes, lustful thoughts

Fantasy lust, looking on the nakedness curse

Harlotry spirits, masturbation spirits

Sexual lust - Fantasy lust, spirits of Rape, molestation and Incest

Sexual abuse; mental abuse, molestation rape

Sexual lust spirits, fornication spirits

Adultery spirit

Demons that came in from watching Pornography

Sexual mind control from porn

Masturbation spirits, craving sex, oral sex, anal sex

Homosexuality, lesbian spirits

Incubus, succubus and marine spirits

Sexual dream spirits, spiritual spouse

Spiritual husband, spiritual wife

COME OUT IN JESUS NAME!

SPIRITS OF JEZABEL AND RELATED SPIRITS

Spirits of jezebel, aggressive spirits

Spirits causing discord, attention seeking spirits

Dominant spirits, emotional outburst / Belittling spirits

Bickering spirits, backbiting spirits

Arrogant spirits, deceiving spirits

Delusion spirits, demanding spirits

Controlling spirits, conditional love

Continuous complaining

Contention, bossy spirits

Failure spirits, disruption spirits

Frustration and fear spirits

Hardness spirits, hopelessness

Hatred spirits, hot temper spirits

Inability to give and receive love

Inadequacy spirits, quick temper

Blame shifting, nagging spirits

Mistrust, distrust, fear, doubt and unbelief!

Lying spirits, Jealousy spirits

Insecurity spirits

Revenge spirits, rebellion spirits

Slander spirits, sexual sin spirits

Complaining spirits, spirits of jezebel

sharp tongue, determined maneuvers

spirits of deception, spirits of control

witchcraft control, flirting spirits

Sexual sin spirits, conniving spirits

COME OUT IN JESUS NAME!

AHAB AND RELATED EVIL SPIRITS

Spirits of Ahab, Ahab personality traits

Poverty spirits, Materialism spirits

Greed spirits, lazy spirits

Passivity spirits, fear of man

Fear of woman, fear of rejection

Lust and ambition for power and recognition

Competitive spirits, covetousness

Greed, won't take responsibility

Passivity demons causing inaction

Passive quitter spirits, apathy spirits

Heaviness, withdraw spirits

Murder spirits, anger spirits

Pouting spirits, childish behavior spirits

False gods, weakness spirits

Subtle spirits, fear of woman

Worldliness spirits, hatred of woman

Rejection, fear of being hurt

Emotional cripple, emotional walls

Deep seated hurts and wounds

Lack of confidence

Macho spirits, Prideful spirits

Manipulating woman, worship of success

Mother domination, loss of manhood

Destruction of the family priesthood

Communication breakdown spirits

Withdraw spirits, escape spirits

Evil spirits of passivity, and compromise

COME OUT IN JESUS NAME!

EVIL SPIRITS OF DEPRESSION

Despair and Discouragement

Hopelessness, and Heaviness

Depression, despair and shame

Fear, anxiety and worry

Suicide, spirits of death and murder

Abortion, fear of death, agreement with death

Suppression and oppression

Smiling on the outside but hurting on the inside

COME OUT IN JESUS NAME!

EVIL SPIRITS OF FEAR

Insomnia, fear of man

Anxiety, worry, unbelief

Fear of sickness, spirit of death

Fear of the dark, fear of failure

Fear of not pleasing man

Fear of flying, paranoia

Fears of accidents

Religious fears, spirits of fear

Phobia, hysteria, fear of rejection

Fear of failure, fear of going to hell

Fear of authority, fear of people

Fear of flying, fear of not being loved

Fear of being wrong

Fear of not having friends

Fear of accidents, fear of animals

Fear of cancer, fear of sickness and disease

Fear of demons, fear of Satan

Fear of the dark, fear of being criticized

Fear of taken advantage of, tormenting fear spirits

Fear of being alone, fear of abuse

Fear of being hurt, fear of the past

Fear of something bad happening

Fear of the future, panic attack spirits

Fear of nothing working out

Fear of heights, fear of rejection

Fear of poverty, fear of falling

Fear of germs, fear of having a heart attach

Fear of heights

COME OUT IN JESUS NAME!

<u>SELF CENTERED SPIRITS</u>

Self-rejection, self-seduction, self-centeredness

Self-importance, Pride and Ahab personality traits

Self-reliance, arrogance and ego

Self-deception, self-Delusion, self-deception

Self-hatred, self-doubt, self-sexual gratification

Self-righteousness, Inferiority, insecurity, and self-exaltation

COME OUT IN JESUS NAME!

EVIL SPIRITS OF PRIDE

Leviathan spirits, spirits of pride, prideful devils

Prideful spirits. worldliness, self-will

Manipulation, hindering spirits, stiff-necked

Rebellion, sorrow, haughtiness, rebellious pride

Me, me, me spirits, soul realm domination, self-deception, witchcraft serpent curse

Anger, argumentative, critical spirits

Frustration spirits, vanity, self-awareness

Impatience spirits, anti-submissiveness

Leviathan spirits, spirits of leviathan

Prideful spirits, mind control spirits, spiritual defilement

False humility, anger, argumentative

Spiritual defilement, critical spirits, false humility

Rejection, gossip spirits, disobedient spirits

COME OUT IN JESUS NAME!

UNCLEAN SPIRITS OF WITCHCRAFT AND KUNDALINI

Witchcraft, spirits, unclean spirits from witches and warlocks

Incantations over your life, medium spirits,

Spirit guide spirits. consulting mediums

Fortune telling spirits, palm reading curses

Involvement with crystal balls

Demons from tarot cards, demons from Astrology

Witchcraft sickness curses, witchcraft curses Hexes and spells

Hypnotism spirits, hand writing analysis

Numerology curses, magic practices

Black magic, white magic

Witchcraft yoga spirits, reincarnation

Witchcraft Buddha curses, witchcraft kundalini

Kundalini transfer, kundalini from worldly music

Kundalini from sexual immorality, kundalini from alcoholism

Kundalini from Marijuana, new age, and satanic worship

COME OUT IN JESUS NAME!

EVIL SPIRITS ATTACKING YOUR EMOTIONS

Emotional death and destruction

Unclean Emotions, emotional damage from sin

Emotional damage from drug addiction

Emotional damage from the occult

Emotional damage from poverty

Emotional damage from pride

Emotional damage from sexual sin

Emotional damage rejection

Emotional damage From rejection by parents,

Emotional damage From self-hatred

Emotional destruction, fear of being hurt

Emotional defeat, emotional Hardness

Emotional fragility. emotional Shut down

Emotional roller coaster, emotional numbness

Emotional imprisonment, emotional outburst

Emotional Instability, bitterness, bottled up emotions

Emotional void and emptiness

Witchcraft curse sent over the emotions

Emotional Hardship, emotionally overwhelmed

Emotional Pain hurts wounds, betrayal

Rejection destroying emotions, emotional Loss of identity

Emotional Torment, emotional torture

Emotional Immaturity, emotional Slavery

Negative emotions, emotionally upset

Emotional Suffocated, emotionally controlled

Emotional manipulation, emotionally dominated

Jezebel emotions, ungodly emotional ties

Emotional Bondage, spiritual ties to past partners

Emotional ties to drugs, nicotine and food

COME OUT IN JESUS NAME!

DEMONS
ATTACKING THE MIND

Mental illness, manic depressive

Depression, suicide, give up spirits, anxiety spirits

Panic attack spirit, worry

Mind racing, mind blanking

Memory loss, confusion, mental torment spirits

Witchcraft curse never the mind

Mental imprisonment, split mind, mental retardation

Mental pain, arrested development

Processing problems in the brain, negative thinking

Fragmented soul spirits, multiple Personalities

OCD, moodiness, disturbed thoughts, distorted thinking

Delusional spirits, phobias, panic attack spirits

Anger outburst, mistrust, distrust, attention deficit

Mental illness, schizophrenia

Depression, hearing of voices, nervous breakdown

Mind racing, mind binding

Mind blanking, disorganized thinking

Bipolar spirits, evil spirits causing a split mind

Mental instability, mental harassment spirits

Double mindedness, nervousness spirits, worry spirits

Fear demons causing lack of faith

Suicidal thoughts, give up spirits

Hopeless spirits, spirits of confusion

Mental torment, negative thoughts

Harassing thoughts, fantasy in the mind

Mental time wasting, irrational thinking

Demons causing you to mull things over and over

Distracted thinking, deceiving spirits in the mind

Unhealthy thinking processes, band over the mind

Chemical imbalances of the mind, low self-image mental abuse

Drawing back spirits, escape and withdraw

Feeling unworthy, unbelief, procrastination

Excuse making spirits, mental distraction

COME OUT IN JESUS NAME!

UNCLEAN SPIRITS OF SHAME

Shame from rejected, shame from being left out

Shame from failure, shame from divorce

Shame from being abused, shame because of sin

Shame through molestation, shame by rape

Shame from masturbation, shame from defeat

Shame from sexual sin, shame by rejection by parents

Embarrassing devils, isolation, frustration

Give up spirits, broken heartedness

Lack of self-love, shame and humiliation

Shame from defeat, shame from sin

Shame from parents, shame from witchcraft

Shame because of looks, shame by sexual sin

Shame from prostitution

COME OUT IN JESUS NAME!

UNCLEAN SPIRITS OF SICKNESS AND DISEASE

All viruses, fungal infection

Lupus, ulcers, lower back pain

Liver problems. hepatitis, shortness of breath

Accident prone spirits, heart problems

Brain sickness, cancer spirits

Breast cancer, pancreatic cancer

Tumors, growths, cyst, seizure spirits

Thyroid spirits, degeneration, high cholesterol

Hearing loss, demons causing Ringing in the ear

Allergy spirits, weakness in the immune system

Spirits of weakness, low blood pressure

High blood pressure, prostate cancer

Deafness, blindness, ALL sickness and disease

Hemorrhoids, arthritis

All pain, gall stones

Cataracts spirits, blindness spirits

Damaged ear drums, unclean spirits causing sickness

Early death curse, varicose veins, barrenness

Infertility, spirits from accidents

Spirits causing ear infection

Demons causing fibromyalgia

Demons causing problems in the lungs

Demons causing tumors

Demons causing memory loss and Alzheimer's

Demons causing nerve disease and boils

Demons causing goiters and scar tissue

Demons causing pneumonia and cancers

Demons causing brain and lung cancer

Demons causing prostate cancer

Demons causing heart problems / Irregular heartbeat

COME OUT IN JESUS NAME!

<u>EVIL SPIRITS OF POVERTY</u>

Loss of prosperity, evil spirits of covetousness

Spirits of greed, slothfulness

Financial disfavor, financial death and destruction

Disobedience causing poverty

Laziness, financial destruction

Financial Idolatry, Following worthless people

Hording money, spirits that came in from not tithing

Material lust, witchcraft poverty

All witchcraft against prosperity

Financial bondage, fear of hunger

Fear of starvation, Fear of financial failure

Disfavor with people, Inherited curses of business

Demons causing financial destruction

Demons causing poverty

Demons causing greed, lack and want

Demons causing doubt concerning success

Demons causing the love of money

Demons causing hatred of giving

Demons that came in from gambling

Demons causing compulsive buying

Demons causing mismanagement of finances

Demons causing the worship of money

COME OUT IN JESUS NAME!

<u>EVIL SPIRITS OF GLUTTONY</u>

Evil spirits of gluttony, evil spirits of Obesity

Inherited gluttony, witchcraft gluttony

Obesity curses, Inherited obesity

Food idolatry, lust for food /Fending for myself, eating when I'm nervous

Eating when I'm idle, eating for self-reward

Overeating for escape, evil spirits of obesity,

Addiction to food, addiction to eat and eat

Demons causing obsession with food

Lust for food, food craving, obesity

Finding comfort in food, food idolatry, food obsession

Anorexia, bulimia, eating disorders

Evil soul ties to food, inherited gluttony

food idolatry, addiction to food, compulsion

Sugar addiction, eating sugar to feel better

Living to eat, obsessed with thoughts of food gorge, binge eating demons

Family traditions of overeating

COME OUT IN JESUS NAME!

<u>VARIETY OF DEMONS TO CAST OUT</u>

Anger, hatred, resentment and unforgiveness

Envy, rebellion, Stubbornness and Controlling

Manipulation, Rejection, Self-rejection and Fear of rejection

Abandonment, Insecurity, Inferiority and Inadequacy

Timidity, Isolation, Passivity and depression

Hopelessness, Suicide, Insomnia and Worry, anxiety & nervousness

Stress, bad habits and disfavor!

Mental illness, paranoia and Confusion,

forgetfulness, doubt and unbelief

Double minded-ness, Mind racing

Mind blanking, disorganized thinking & speech!

Lying, stealing and pride!

Self-righteousness, self-importance and hard to admit wrong!

Gossip, sorrow and demons causing soul wounds!

Sadness, guilt and condemnation!

Shame, self-hatred and self-pity

Mental abuse, emotional abuse and physical abuse!

Verbal abuse, nicotine, alcohol, drugs and gluttony, lust, fornication, adultery, Homosexuality!

Pornography, abortion, and all sexual sin!

Fear, phobia, doubt, laziness, sloth

Word curses, poverty, loss of prosperity!

Cults, witchcraft, Ouija board, palm reading and tarot cards, Deafness, blindness, cataracts and diabetes

Chapter 10

HOW TO WALK IN FREEDOM!

WE WALK IN FREEDOM BY THE HOLY GHOST

I had a dream years ago that I was being watched and protected by this person, and every time I did something wrong or my enemies would try to kill me, he worked it out for my good! When a circumstance or an attack arose, he would use his supernatural power to maneuver my win, he was always there and he revealed to me that he would always be the reason I never lose or die! I was always a step ahead of my enemies because of him! *He's the Mighty 3rd person of the Godhead, he's the Helper and Comforter that indwells the believer! He's the eternal, wonderful Holy Spirit!*

'John 14:15-17 "If you love Me, keep My commandments. And I will pray the Father, and He will give you another Helper, that He may abide

with you forever— the Spirit of truth, whom the world cannot receive, because it neither sees Him nor knows Him; but you know Him, for He dwells with you and will be in you.

John 15:26 'But when the Comforter is come, whom I will send unto you from the Father, even the Spirit of truth, which proceedeth from the Father, he shall testify of me'

John 16:7 'Nevertheless I tell you the truth. It is to your advantage that I go away; for if I do not go away, the Helper will not come to you; but if I depart, I will send Him to you.'

You have the same Holy Ghost, JESUS and the apostles had, the same eternal life, the same righteousness, the same gospel, the same ability, the same POWER, the same GRACE, the same WORD, the same AUTHORITY, the same shed BLOOD, the same weapons of our warfare, the same WISDOM, the Father has no favorites! *And now your fellowship with the Holy Spirit will determine the trajectory of your life!*

2 Corinthians 13:14 YLT 'the grace of the Lord Jesus Christ, and the love of God, and the fellowship of the Holy Spirit, is with you all! Amen.' The Greek word for fellowship is 'Koinonia' which literally means 'fellowship, association, community, communion, and intimacy, so from this verse we learn *'Our fellowship, association and communion with the Holy Ghost will determine our freedom, and what spiritual gifts are activated in our lives! The Holy Ghost needs to be the most important person in our life and now we have unlimited intimacy, communion, and fellowship with him!* ***Zechariah 4:6 'So he answered and said to me: "This is the word of the LORD to Zerubbabel: Not by might nor by power, but by My Spirit,' Says the LORD of hosts'*** The Holy Spirit is intimately involved in every detail of our lives and he engages us when we need him the most! In 2015 while in a demonic storm, I laid on my ex-wife's couch and as I laid there in the early morning Jan 26th I realized I wasn't awake and I wasn't asleep. Then I heard an audible voice speaking out of my spirit-man saying **'I'M HERE, I'M HERE, I LOVE YOU'** again he said **'I'M HERE, I'M HERE, I LOVE YOU!'**

I could literally feel his voice pulsating out of my spirit! Wow, I was blown away by the strategic, glorious, life-changing and graceful Ministry of the Holy Spirit, that at my worst, he knew exactly what I needed to hear to keep me on track in obedience to the CALL of God on my life! *That was a LIFE CHANGING encounter with the wonderful Holy Spirit that brought this scripture to life!* **1 John 4:4 Young's Literal Translation 'Ye -- of God ye are, little children, and ye have overcome them; because greater is He who [is] in you, than he who is in the world"** I later realized, Jan 26th was the day I was born again in 2008, and it would be the same day, a year later in 2016 that I would celebrate graduating a sales rookie program that was a life changing accomplishment, launching my career as an outside sales rep that radically changed my life and Ministry! *God is into small details, dates and numbers, he wrote a whole book called Numbers and he has ways of showing you, he's watching you; he loves you and he's at work in and for you! Praise God for the eternal helper, the Mighty 3RD Person of the trinity 'the Holy Spirit' that makes it impossible for us to fail!*

THE BAPTISM OF THE HOLY GHOST AND FIRE

Deuteronomy 4:24 "For the Lord thy God is a consuming fire, even a jealous God."

Deuteronomy 9:3 "But understand that today the LORD your God goes across ahead of you as a consuming fire; He will destroy them and subdue them before you. And you will drive them out and annihilate them swiftly, as the LORD has told you.'

Your enemy and all his cohorts are afraid of the fire of God, they tremble when the fire of God is in operation! The fire of God burns wickedness; burns demon yokes; burns demon sickness; burns evil influences! The fire of God heals the mind, burns away lies, destroys curses and witchcraft spells! The fire of God burns up all his foes! *Psalms 97:1-3 "Jehovah is King! Let all the earth rejoice! Tell the farthest islands to be glad. Clouds and darkness surround him. Righteousness and justice are the foundation of his throne. Fire goes forth before him and burns up all his foes'* Jesus Christ the Son of God; came to reveal and release the fire of God! He came to destroy the works of the devil by the fire of God. He came to set you ablaze and reveal the key to success and victory! *Luke 12:49 "I have come to set the world on fire"* Jesus came to set the Church ablaze for the Glory of God! *Acts 2:3-4 "And there appeared unto them cloven tongues like as of fire, and it sat upon each of them. And they were all filled with the Holy Ghost, and began to speak with other tongues, as the Spirit gave them utterance.'* The fire of God will be a channel for the Holy Ghost to speak to you! You will hear the voice of God louder than ever; and you will ACT on the small still voice of the Holy Spirit! He will show you Visions and dreams! As you are now led by the Spirit of fire! *Heb 6:4-5 "For it is impossible for those who were once enlightened, and have tasted the heavenly gift, and have become partakers of the Holy Spirit, and have tasted the good word of God and the powers of the age to come'* The word for enlightened in the Greek is 'fotidzo' which literally means to give light, to shine, to enlighten, light up, to bring to light, to give understanding! *Luke 3:16 "John answered them all, saying, "I baptize you with water, but he who is mightier than I is coming, the strap of whose sandals I am not worthy to untie. He will baptize you with the Holy Spirit and fire"* The fire of God gives you passion for the WORD of God, the WORD ignites the fire of God, the WORD is the lighter fluid for the fire and all things are possible now by the fire of God! You will see things and do things you would have never imagined by the fire of God! The WORD of God on your mouth is like a flame of fire being released against your enemies in the realm of the spirit! *'Jeremiah 23:19 "Is not my word like fire saith the LORD?* The fire of God will destroy all wickedness, darkness, and evil influence in you and those you minister too! Do not neglect the fire of God, add it to your arsenal of divine weapons to fulfill the call of God on your life! *'Psalms 104:4 "Who maketh his angels spirits; his ministers a flaming fire'* *We receive the fire of God and the baptism of the Holy Ghost by faith! Faith is simply what you speak with your mouth, what you believe in your heart and your actions!*

Mark 11:23 "For assuredly, I say to you, whoever says to this mountain, 'Be removed and be cast into the sea,' and does not doubt in his heart, but believes that those things he says will be done, he will have whatever he says.

Romans 10:9-10 "that if you confess with your mouth the Lord Jesus and believe in your heart that God has raised Him from the dead, you will be saved. For with the heart one believes unto righteousness, and with the mouth confession is made unto salvation.

James 2:20-22 "But do you want to know, O foolish man, that faith without works is dead? -- Was not Abraham our Father justified by works when he offered Isaac his son on the altar? Do you see that faith was working together with his works, and by works faith was made perfect?

HOW TO RECEIVE THE POWER OF GOD AND TONGUES OF FIRE!

Acts 1:8 'But you shall receive power, after that the Holy Ghost is come on you: and you shall be witnesses to me both in Jerusalem, and in all Judaea, and in Samaria, and to the uttermost part of the earth. First, we ask God by faith; God will never deny us what we ask according to his will. ***Luke 11:11-13, If a son asks for bread from any Father among you, will he give him a stone? Or if he asks for a fish, will he give him a serpent instead of a fish? Or if he asks for an egg, will he offer him a scorpion? If you then, being evil, know how to give good gifts to your children, how much more will your heavenly Father give the Holy Spirit to those who ask Him!"*** Now we believe; after we ask for it by faith; then we believe it is God's will for us! ***Mark 9:23 "if thou canst believe—all things are possible to him that believes?*** BY FAITH NOW WE BEGIN TO SPEAK IN TONGUES! We don't wait for God to move our mouth for us; we begin to speak in tongues! The bible says the early Church 'began to speak in tongues' ***Acts 2:4, and they were all filled with the Holy Ghost, and began to speak with***

other tongues, as the Spirit gave them utterance."

ACTIVATION

<u>3 KEYS TO RECEIVING THE BAPTISM OF THE HOLY GHOST</u>

1. What you say; ask God to release his fire in your life right now in the NAME of JESUS! Do it now boldly!
2. We believe he's doing it! Say I believe I'm receiving the fire of God by faith! – say 'I believe it is God's will I receive the power of God in my life now!
3. You're action; now begin to speak in tongues of fire; quickly by faith, were not waiting for angels to descend from heaven and move our mouth for us and were not worried about how we feel!

DO IT NOW, start worshipping God in tongues! Now speak in tongues every day, and when you do, you're building up your faith. *'Jude 1:20 But you, beloved, building yourselves up on your most holy faith, praying in the Holy Spirit'* When you do this, you are confusing demons, because only God can understand you and you are speaking directly to him! *1 Corinthians 14:2-3 'For he that speaketh in an unknown tongue speaketh not unto men, but unto God: for no man understandeth him; howbeit in the spirit he speaketh mysteries.* You are also being strengthened, encouraged and edified when you pray in tongues! Why wouldn't we do this all day? *Verse 3 The one who speaks in a tongue edifies himself'.*

WE WALK IN FREEDOM BY DOING THE WORD OF GOD

James 1:22 "But be ye doers of the word, and not hearers only, deceiving your own selves. You know the WORD, you speak the WORD, and you memorize the WORD! You do the WORD, you know what the WORD says about the enemy; you love the WORD! The WORD is your foundation in a pandemic, in a storm, in a crisis; in all adversity, the WORD is a lamp unto your feet!

Hebrews 4:12 'For the word of God is quick, and powerful, and sharper than any two-edged sword, piercing even to the dividing asunder of soul and spirit, and of the joints and marrow, and is a discerner of the thoughts and intents of the heart.'

Isaiah 55:11 'So shall my word be that goeth forth out of my mouth: it shall not return unto me void, but it shall accomplish that which I please, and it shall prosper in the thing whereto I sent it.'

Psalms 107:20 "He sent his word, and healed them, and delivered them from their destructions."

THE SWORD OF THE SPIRIT IS THE WORD OF GOD

Ephesians 6:10-17 'Finally, my brethren, be strong in the Lord and in the power of His might. Put on the whole armor of God, 'that you may be able to stand against the wiles of the devil' (Methodias –trickery) For we do not wrestle against flesh and blood, but against principalities, against powers, against the rulers of the darkness of this age, against spiritual hosts of wickedness in the heavenly places, Therefore take up the whole armor of God, that you may be able to withstand in the evil day, and having done all, to stand. Stand therefore, having girded your waist with truth, having put on the breastplate of righteousness, and having shod your feet with the preparation of the gospel of peace; above all, taking the shield of faith with which you will be able to quench all the fiery darts of the wicked one. And take the helmet of salvation, and the sword of the Spirit, which is the word of God.' The Greek word Paul used here for word is 'Rhema' the Sword of the Spirit is the 'Rhema' of God, this word literally means 'the Spoken-word' an utterance, a saying of any sort, as a message 'any sound produced by the voice' The Bible sitting on your shelf, isn't the Sword of the Spirit! *The Sword of the Spirit is when you take the WORD of God and decree, speak,*

241

shout, utter and release a sound from your mouth! Speaking and declaring the PROMISES of God by the WORD of God!

God placed his WORD in your mouth, your mouth is now a weapon in the KINGDOM of God! ***Isaiah 59:21 "As for Me," says the Lord, "this is My covenant with them: My Spirit who is upon you, and My words which I have put in your mouth, shall not depart from your mouth."*** So many times were not looking at the WORD as the solution! We're asking God to fix everything the way we want it done! Meanwhile, if we just went to the WORD, it's all there! Grace, wisdom, divine power, joy, peace, victory, strength, freedom, and divine healing! ***Psalms 119:28 "My soul melteth for heaviness: strengthen thou me according unto thy word.'***

WE NEED TO RADICALLY DO, ACT ON, AND EXECUTE GOD'S HOLY WORD!

The WORD of God is the will of God, and the will of God is the WORD of God! As we walk in

FREEDOM, we grow and conquer by being a DOER of the WORD or the WILL of God, the below scripture declares the importance of submission to the WORD of God or the will of God!

Matthew 7:21 "Not everyone who says to Me, 'Lord, Lord,' shall enter the kingdom of heaven, but he who does the will of My Father in heaven."

Matthew 12:50 "For whosoever shall do the will of my Father which is in heaven, the same is my brother'

As the people of God, were passionate about the WORD of God and we know that genuine freedom and TRANSFORMATION comes by DOING the WORD! There is no blessing in disobedience, there is no favor, divine healing or deliverance in disobedience! That's why it is imperative we are fully aware of what the WORD requires of us! And that we are DOERS of it! The Christ declared if you are not a DOER of his WORD your house is built on sand and great will be its fall.

'Matthew 7:24-27 "Therefore whoever hears these sayings of Mine, and DOES them, I will liken him to a wise man

who built his house on the rock: and the rain descended, the floods came, and the winds blew and beat on that house; and it did not fall, for it was founded on the rock. "But everyone who hears these sayings of Mine, and does not do them, will be like a foolish man who built his house on the sand: and the rain descended, and the floods came, and the winds blew and beat ono that house, and it fell and great was the fall of it.'

James 1:22 "But be ye doers of the word, and not hearers only, deceiving your own selves.'

Joel 2:11 "And Jehovah hath given forth His voice before His force, For very great [is] His camp, For mighty [is] the doer of His word."

John 8:31-32 "Jesus, therefore, said unto the Jews who believed in him, 'If ye may remain (Or DO) in my word, truly my disciples ye are, and ye shall know the truth, and the truth shall make you free.'

JESUS has the solution and the perfect way to fight the devil! And he wants to teach us how to do it, it's very simple, we just have to do what God says to do; JESUS is an example for us! We need to fight the devil the same way JESUS did! ***Matthew 4:1-4 "Then was Jesus led up of the Spirit into the wilderness to be tempted of the devil. And when he had fasted forty days and forty nights, he was afterward an hungred. And when the tempter came to him, he said, If thou be the Son of God, command that these stones be made bread. But he answered and said, It is written, Man shall not live by bread alone, but by every word that proceedeth out of the mouth of God.'*** How did Jesus fight the devil? He said *'It is written'* That's right, he repeatedly said *'It is written'* 'Now that's your answer for the rest of your life! ***Matthew 4:5-7 "Then the devil taketh him up into the holy city, and setteth him on a pinnacle of the temple, And saith unto him, If thou be the Son of God, cast thyself down: for it is written, He shall give his angels charge concerning thee: and in their hands they shall bear thee up, lest at*** *any time thou dash thy foot against a stone. Jesus said unto him, It is written again, Thou shalt not tempt the Lord thy God"* The devil will bombard your mind and give you all kinds of excuses why you're not going to receive God's promise, but if you'll just stand steadfast and Say 'IT IS WRITTEN' The devil is crazy, he won't quit the first time! *Matthew 4:8-11 "Again, the devil taketh him up into an exceeding high mountain, and sheweth him all the kingdoms of the world, and the glory of them; And saith unto him, All these things will I give thee, if thou wilt fall down and worship me. Then saith Jesus unto him, Get thee hence, Satan: for it is written, Thou shalt worship the Lord thy God, and him only shalt thou serve. Then the devil leaveth him, and, behold, angels came and ministered unto him."* Remember the devil always comes back, he hasn't been thrown into the lake of fire yet, so you will need the WORD as long as you live on earth! Always remember to say 'IT IS WRITTEN!' when confronting the devil and his lies, then verse 11 tells us what happened for JESUS and what will happen in your life!

Matthew 4:11 "Then the devil left Him, and behold, angels came and ministered to Him.'

WE WALK IN FREEDOM BY PRAYER

Prayer is how we get the call and assignment! Prayer is how Heavens GOVT the KINGDOM of God effects, changes, disrupts, and penetrates the earth! Prayer is how heaven invades the earth! God will show you a vision when you pray to help you! At the phoenix dream center in 2010 after fasting and praying, I saw 'ugly demon faces' in the spirit-realm, God revealing to me; who the real enemy is and that it's a spiritual battle, not a carnal-fleshly one! Prayer is how the Holy Spirit will guide you, speak to you, promote you, humble you, change you, and reveal the Christ to you! It shows him you're ready to hear from him! You're preparing yourself to hear and obey! Prayer is the foundation of the New Testament Church, and we must change our mind set about prayer! In 2011 the ANGEL of the LORD sent from the presence of ALMIGHTY God visited me and I heard an audible voice communicate my earthly calling and purpose!

I have literally never been the same since that encounter with the Spirit of God because I woke up that morning seeking the KINGDOM of God in prayer! When you pray, your mouth will be large over your enemies, like Hannah in *1 Samuel 2:1 the bible says "Hannah prayed and said, "My heart rejoiceth in the Lord; mine horn is exalted in the Lord. My mouth hath been large over my enemies!"* Your mouth will be large over Satan, large over disease, large over poverty, large over fear, large over sin, large over witchcraft, and large over death!* When Paul had his encounter with the Christ, he was humbled and blinded by Christ in order to get his attention! The Bible says Paul was praying and saw a vision, God speaking to Ananias. *Acts 9:11 "Get up! the Lord told him. Go to the house of Judas on Straight Street and ask for a man from Tarsus named Saul, for he is praying, and in a vision he has seen a man named Ananias come and place his hands on him to restore his sight."* A man named Cornelius who always prayed to God was the first Gentile to whom God brings the glorious gospel! *Acts 10:1-5 'there was a certain man in Caesarea called*

Cornelius, a centurion of what was called the Italian Regiment, a devout man and one who feared God with all his household, who gave alms generously to the people, and prayed to God always. About the ninth hour of the day he saw clearly in a vision an angel of God coming in and saying to him, "Cornelius! And when he observed him, he was afraid, and said, "What is it, lord?" So he said to him, "Your prayers and your alms have come up for a memorial before God. Now send men to Joppa, and send for Simon whose surname is Peter' Peter was praying when he got the call to preach the glorious gospel to the gentiles! And God shows him gentiles are no longer unclean! *Acts 10:9-13 "the next day, as they went on their journey and drew near the city, Peter went up on the housetop to pray, about the sixth hour. Then he became very hungry and wanted to eat; but while they made ready, he fell into a trance and saw heaven opened and an object like a great sheet bound at the four corners, descending to him and let down to the earth. In it were all kinds of four-footed animals of the earth, wild beasts, creeping things, and birds of the air. And a voice came to him, "Rise, Peter; kill and eat."* Verse 19, the Spirit sent the gentiles to receive the gospel, verse 28 Peter tells Cornelius *"And he said unto them, Ye know how that it is an unlawful thing for a man that is a Jew to keep company, or come unto one of another nation; but God hath shewed me that I should not call any man common or unclean."* All because Cornelius and Peter were submitted to a lifestyle of prayer. In these end times 'God is revealing, mysteries, secrets, knowledge, great and mighty things that we would have never known unless we had cried out to him in prayer!' *Jeremiah 33:3 'Call unto me, and I will answer thee, and show thee great and mighty things, which thou knowest not."* One Christian can have a greater revelation of the Christ and accomplish more than another Christian because of prayer! We determine how deep we go with God; you can be dedicated, determined, passionate, and persistent in the KINGDOM of God, or you can be afraid, lazy, and carnal, bound to natural circumstances! King David knew the importance of prayer and crying out to God!

Psalms 30:1-3 'I will extol You, O Lord, for You have lifted me up, And have not let my foes rejoice over me. O Lord my God, I cried out to You, And You healed me. O Lord, You brought my soul up from the grave; You have kept me alive, that I should not go down to the pit.

Psalms 119:145-146 said 'I cry out with my whole heart; Hear me, O Lord! I will keep Your statutes. I cry out to You; Save me, and I will keep Your testimonies.

The Holy Spirit will help you pray when you don't know how to! When we submit our tongue to prayer, when we live a disciplined life, determined to pray persistently! When we shout unto God with a voice of triumph in prayer! When we pray in tongues, it may sound weird in the natural realm, but in the Spirit realm you're breaking strongholds and EXPANDING the KINGDOM of God! You're obtaining the perfect will of God and someone else is praying with you, through you, and

for you to the Father! ***Romans 8:26-27
'Likewise the Spirit also helps in our
weaknesses. For we do not know what
we should pray for as we ought,
but the Spirit Himself makes
intercession for us with groanings
which cannot be uttered. Now He who
searches the hearts knows what the
mind of the Spirit is, because He makes
intercession for the saints according
to the will of God.'*** We need to be able to
change our circumstances and our destiny through
prayer! When we draw nigh, he draws nigh to us,
when we pray in the Spirit, he intercedes to the
Father the perfect will of God *(the idea is as we
pray in tongues, he's interceding to the
Father on our behalf).* He's helping you
OVERCOME all the weaknesses of the past that
Satan keeps using against you! That word 'helps' in
verse 26 comes from a Greek word that literally
means *'to take hold together with you against,
to help in obtaining'* He's going to take hold
together with you against fear, against poverty,
against evil spirits, against passivity, against
compromise, against defeat! He's going to help you
obtain sanity, victory, and divine healing! He's going
to help you obtain the Call of God, prosperity,

divine joy, and all the promises Christ died to provide you with! And because you're a persistent man or woman of prayer; then God will work all things together for good in your life! '**Romans 8:28 'And we know that all things work together for good to those who love God, to those who are the called according to His purpose.** When we pray, we are CRUSHING hell and saying, 'NO MORE ROTTEN DEVIL.' You can't do those things anymore; you are exposed; you MUST let my family go, let my children go! And because you are the righteousness of God, in right standing with God through the Christ, your petitions and prayers will be answered for the GLORY of JESUS! '**James 5:16 The effectual fervent prayer of a righteous man availeth much"** Prayer is releasing the POWER of God in any given situation! *The POWER of God is in the WORD of God, when you pray the WORD of God, we release the POWER of God into the spirit-realm which will influence, change, and shape your circumstance in the natural realm!* God honors his WORD; prayer is a spirit-realm action, not a mental exercise; prayer should always be in the spirit! ***Ephesians 6:17-18 And take the helmet of salvation, and the*** *sword of the Spirit, which is the word of God: Praying always with all prayer and supplication in the Spirit, and watching thereunto with all perseverance and supplication for all saints."*

WE WALK IN FREEDOM BY PRAISE

Now that we have been radically delivered, we walk this out in PRAISE like Jeremiah did! *Jeremiah 20:13 "Sing to the Lord, praise the Lord! For He has delivered the soul of the needy one From the hand of evildoers.'* When you have seen the goodness of God in your life, when you have seen the Holy Spirit annihilate the evil powers of Satan and set your mind free, break and eradicate all generational curses, and when you can look back and say, I can't even recognize myself! ALL YOU WILL WANT TO DO IS PRAISE THE LORD JESUS LIKE KING DAVID. *'Psalms 150:1-6 'Praise ye the Lord. Praise God in his sanctuary: praise him in the firmament of his power. Praise him for his mighty acts:*

praise him according to his excellent greatness. Praise him with the sound of the trumpet: praise him with the psaltery and harp. Praise him with the timbrel and dance: praise him with stringed instruments and organs. Praise him upon the loud cymbals: praise him upon the high sounding cymbals. Let everything that hath breath praise the Lord. Praise ye the Lord.' The devil wants you isolated, but the best place to be is in the congregation of the saints praising God! The enemy says don't go to Church, because when you're with the people of God Praising God, the atmosphere will change your life! *Psalms 149:1-9, "Praise ye the Lord. Sing unto the Lord a new song, and his praise in the congregation of saints.'*

PRAISE BRINGS TRIUMPH OVER DEMON POWERS!

Psalms 149:1-2 Praise the Lord! Sing to the Lord a new song, And His praise in the assembly of saints. Let Israel

rejoice in him that made him: let the children of Zion be joyful in their King!
The word that is translated rejoice is a Hebrew word that is also translated triumph. He is talking about being triumphant through the act of PRAISE! In other words, there is a type of PRAISE that defeats the devil, Hallelujah! When you start praising, you begin triumphing! In the Old Testament, they didn't have the blood of JESUS as a weapon; they didn't have the NAME of JESUS as a weapon, but they did have praise! When Saul was troubled by an evil spirit; the only way they knew to help him was to have David play on a harp and sing praise, then the evil spirit departed from King Saul! How much greater should our praise be for the RISEN Christ and what he has done for us! *We have the BLOOD of the EXALTED Christ, we have the NAME of JESUS, now we add praise to the divine-arsenal of weapons, and you will see the VICTORY God has promised you!* God LOVES when his people praise because it's an action of humility! **Verses 3-6 "Let them praise His name with the dance; Let them sing praises to Him with the timbrel and harp. For the Lord takes pleasure in His people; He will beautify the humble with salvation. Let the**

saints be joyful in glory; Let them sing aloud on their beds. Let the high praises of God be in their mouth, and a two-edged sword in their hand." The two-edged sword is the WORD of God. Your mouth was created to praise and speak the WORD! When you combine praise and the WORD, darkness retreats! The term "high praises of God" here means to "exalt God, to glorify God, to magnify God out of your heart. The high praise of God signifies praise that comes from deep within us, running out of our hearts! It is the expression of exultation, magnification, and glorification of God. Those are the HIGH PRAISES of God. *Verse 7 "To execute vengeance upon the heathen, and punishments upon the peoples."* This has a spiritual meaning to it, he is talking here about the satanic nations, the principalities and powers of the devil! The devil has nations of demons set up in the heavenly realm. He says we are going to obtain revenge upon these nations through our praise and execute punishment on the peoples! Do you realize that demons are punished and tormented by our praise? I want you to understand what your praise does in the spirit realm! A demon cannot exist in that environment, he cannot function in that environment! It would be like a human trying to exist where there is no air! When we praise, we are creating an atmosphere where the devil cannot operate! Demons have tormented us long enough, and through praise we turn the tables and torment them! ***Verse 8 'To bind their kings with chains, and their nobles with fetters of iron"*** That word bind means to "keep in prison" or to restrain by governmental authority or command. When you bind these spiritual enemies, you are imprisoning them and restraining them by governmental authority! Now what government is he talking about? the KINGDOM of God! We represent the KINGDOM of God, and we function in the authority of God's KINGDOM, so we have the power through our commands, backed by KINGDOM authority to bind the nobles and the kings with chains and fetters of iron. ***Verse 9 "To execute upon them the judgment written: this honour have all his saints. Praise ye the Lord.***" This honor have all the saints, means that you can defeat the enemy with the weapon of praise, every one of us can do it, with no exceptions! Praise causes shame and confusion in the enemy's camp! ***Psalms 70:2-4 "Let them be ashamed and confounded Who seek my life; Let them be turned back*** *and confused Who desire my hurt. ³ Let them be turned back because of their shame, Who say, "Aha, aha!" ⁴ Let all those who seek You rejoice and be glad in You; And let those who love Your salvation say continually, "Let God be magnified!"* The praise of the people of God will cause the adversary to be clothed in shame and disgrace! ***Psalms 109:29-30 "Let my accusers be clothed with shame, And let them cover themselves with their own disgrace as with a mantle. ³⁰ I will greatly praise the Lord with my mouth; Yes, I will praise Him among the multitude.'*** We need to be a people of PRAISE, RADICAL, God-fearing, DESPERATE, and UNCEASING, LIMITLESS PRAISE! PRAISE will shut the devil's filthy mouth; and silence the satanic kingdom! ***Psalms 8:2 'From the mouths of children and infants You have ordained praise on account of Your adversaries, to silence the enemy and avenger'***

SATAN HATES OUR WORSHIP

So, there were 3 Archangels in Heaven. Michael, who handles prayer, and when Daniel prayed, Michael showed up! Lucifer, who oversaw worship, and Gabriel, who brought the word and messages to the people of God; you remember he spoke to Mary about the Messiah. When Lucifer fell from Heaven, 1/3 of the angels joined his failed attempt to usurp the throne of God, which means there's 2/3 on our side! ***Ezekiel 28:12-13 "Thus says the Lord God: "You were the seal of perfection, Full of wisdom and perfect in beauty. You were in Eden, the garden of God; Every precious stone was your covering: The sardius, topaz, and diamond, Beryl, onyx, and jasper, Sapphire, turquoise, and emerald with gold. The workmanship of your timbrels and pipes Was prepared for you on the day you were created"*** Satan was made of actual instruments 'timbrels and pipes' A timbrel is a small hand drum or tambourine, which cover percussion instruments, pipes are wind instruments. So, who did God replace Lucifer with?

The end times Church of God! He replaced Lucifer with you; you were actually born with 3 kinds of instruments!

1 - String instruments, 'your vocal cords to Sing and worship!'

2- Percussion instruments, 'hands to clap and glorify JESUS!'

3- Wind instruments, 'Your lungs to shout unto God with a VOICE of TRIUMPH!

That's why he hates you, and that's why PRAISE is so important in our lives!

<u>WE WALK IN FREEDOM BY SUFFERING</u>

PRAISE God for adversity and affliction because in it we see JESUS and hear his VOICE! ***Isaiah 30:20-21 Though he give you the bread of adversity and water of affliction, yet he will be with you to teach you—with your own eyes you will see your Teacher. And if you leave God's paths and go astray, you will hear a voice***

***behind you say "No, this is the way;
walk here."*** The real gospel of the KINGDOM
will always include suffering; no one wants to hear
that word, but in order to get into the KINGDOM
we have to suffer! It may hurt, with pressure on all
sides, it will be difficult, but it will be worth it!

***Matthew 7:13-14 'Enter by the narrow
gate; for wide is the gate and broad
is the way that leads to destruction,
and there are many who go in by it
'Because narrow is the gate and
difficult is the way which leads to life,
and there are few who find it'***

***2 Tim 2:3 'You therefore must endure
hardship as a good soldier of Jesus
Christ.'***

***2 Timothy 1:8 'So do not be ashamed of
the testimony of our Lord, or of me, His
prisoner. Instead, join me in suffering
for the gospel by the power of God.'***

God would rather you suffer now in surrendering
control over to him than suffer for eternity! Crisis,
afflictions, and hardships are the processes God
uses to build you because when you get up, you
establish FREEDOM! It's the action of

OVERCOMING the bad habit, OVERCOMING the trials, OVERCOMING the Sin of the past, falling, learning, and growing, one spiritual inch after another! But it starts with suffering because you're saying, 'No devil,' I'm not going to do what's easy! No more shortcuts, no more quick fixes, you rotten devil! *1 Peter 4:1 'Therefore, since Christ suffered for us in the flesh, arm yourselves also with the same mind, for he who has suffered in the flesh has ceased from sin'* Through suffering we learn obedience! The trials, tests, afflictions, calamities, and proving to teach us obedience and keep us obedient! If the divine Master JESUS learned obedience through suffering, guess who else will learn obedience through suffering? *Hebrews 5:8 "Though he were a Son, yet learned he obedience by the things which he suffered.'*

WE WALK IN FREEDOM BY STAYING HUMBLE

God opposes the proud, pride will keep you bound, pride hurts, it never helps! Pride says I got this under control! How do we humble ourselves? We cast our cares upon him, instead of trying to control everything! *1 Peter 5:5-7 'Likewise you younger people, submit yourselves to your elders. Yes, all of you be submissive to one another, and be clothed with humility, for "God resists the proud, But gives grace to the humble." Therefore humble yourselves under the mighty hand of God, that He may exalt you in due time, How do we do that? casting all your care upon Him, for He cares for you.'* God resist the proud, and will resist you, humble you, and allow things to happen to break you! *James 4:6 'God resists the proud, But gives grace to the humble.'*

<u>WE WALK IN FREEDOM WHEN WE DIE TO SELF</u>

Gal 2:20 'I am crucified with Christ: nevertheless I live; yet not I, but Christ liveth in me.'

Rom 6:4-6 'Therefore we were buried with Him through baptism into death, that just as Christ was raised from the dead by the glory of the Father, even so we also should walk in newness of life, For if we have been united together in the likeness of His death, certainly we also shall be in the likeness of His resurrection.

Luke 9:23 'If any man will come after me, let him deny himself, and take up his cross daily, and follow me'

Matthew 10:39 "He that findeth his life shall lose it: and he that loseth his life for my sake shall find it.

Romans 12:1 "I beseech you therefore brethren, by the MERCIES of God --- 'that you present your bodies as a living sacrifice'

<u>WE WALK IN FREEDOM BY KINGDOM AUTHORITY</u>

Luke 10:19 'lo, I give to you the authority to tread upon serpents and scorpions, and on all the power of the enemy, and nothing by any means

shall hurt you.' The Greek word for tread here is pateo, It's a verb, an action word which means to trample and crush with the feet, it means 'to advance by setting foot upon, to tread upon' to TRAMPLE and TREAD-DOWN UNDERFOOT! So from this verse we learn *'With the authority delegated to us in the NAME of JESUS; we advance the KINGDOM of God by setting foot upon the enemy, we trample and tread-down underfoot evil spirits, and crush with the feet all the power of the enemy.'* Authority is the Greek word 'exousia' which literally means 'the power of government' Heavens GOVT has given you power! It means the power of him whose commands must be submitted to by others and obeyed, So when the command goes out the enemy must obey you! 'Exousia' also means, the power of judicial decisions, you're a representative of KING JESUS and you've decided to do away with and CONQUER the enemy's kingdom! ***Matthew 28:18-19 "All authority has been given to Me in heaven and on earth. Go ye therefore, and teach all nations, baptizing them in the name of the Father, and of the Son, and of the Holy Ghost."***

Here the divine Master says, all authority was given unto him, then by saying 'GO' he's delegated that same AUTHORITY to us, the end times army of God, DO YOU BELIEVE IT?

WE WALK IN FREEDOM BY THE GRACE OF GOD

The grace of God is going to be your strength when the enemy strikes and tries to derail you. YOU'RE NOT GOING TO BE MOVED BECAUSE THE GRACE OF GOD IS WONDERFULLY AT WORK IN AND THROUGH YOU! Grace stands *for* 'Gifts received at Christs expense' Meaning he already paid for your freedom! And now we walk it out by the GRACE of God which will enable you to CONQUER in difficult times! *2 Cor 12:9 'And He said to me, "My grace is sufficient for you, for My strength is made perfect in weakness. Therefore most gladly I will rather boast in my infirmities, that the power of Christ may rest upon me.'* The Greek word for grace is "Charis" which means "divine influence upon the heart, and its reflection in your life' this wonderful word literally means 'God's

EVANGELIST PETER VALENZUELA

enablement and earthly blessings and wealth which are due to divine goodness are yours now! It's the extremely diverse powers and gifts granted to Christians! Grace guarantees successful spiritual warfare and causes you to REIGN on the earth! ***Romans 5:17 "For if by one man's offense death reigned by one, much more those who receive abundance of grace and the gift of righteousness shall reign in life by One, Jesus Christ.'*** The Apostle Paul knew how important GRACE was to be successful in spiritual warfare!

1 Corinthians 15:10 "But by the grace of God I am what I am: and his grace which was bestowed upon me was not in vain; but I laboured more abundantly than they all: yet not I, but the grace of God which was with me."

Ephesians 2:6-7 "and did raise [us] up together, and did seat [us] together in the heavenly [places] in Christ Jesus, that He might show, in the ages that are coming, the exceeding riches of His grace in kindness toward us in Christ Jesus."

Chapter 11

WILL YOU BECOME A DELIVERER?

YOU'RE AN END TIME WARRIOR LIKE GIDEON!

In Matthew 10:8 JESUS speaking of deliverance said, *'**Freely you have received, freely give'*** meaning now God wants to do through us, what he did for us! God will deliver you, in order to TRAIN YOU, EQUIP-YOU, and AUTHORIZE-YOU 'to become a DELIVERER!' Since I received deliverance in 2011, I have been ANOINTED in this Ministry, to eradicate Satan's kingdom; and cast out devils! I have seen a multitude of hundreds of people wonderfully made whole through the ministry of deliverance! There is no such thing as receiving deliverance for relief only and then living a carnal life! We must understand God wants to release the Children's Bread in our lives, so we can help others receive it! Gideon's name was changed to Jerubbaal, Gideon was delivered from the Midianites in order to become a deliverer! ***1 Samuel 12:11 'And the LORD sent Jerubbaal, and Bedan, and Jephthah,*** *and Samuel, and delivered you out of the hand of your enemies on every side, and ye dwelled safe.'* The story of Gideon is captured in Judges chapter 6. Gideon didn't see himself the way JEHOVAH saw him, so he sent the ANGEL of the LORD to reveal to Gideon who he really was 'A MIGHTY ONE' *Judges 6:12 "And the angel of the Lord appeared unto him, and said unto him, The Lord is with thee, thou mighty man of valour"* Why was Gideon a Mighty man of valour? Because JEHOVAH was with him; well guess who else JEHOVAH is with? Yes, you and you are an end-times 'Mighty Man and Woman of valour!' In the Young's Literal, the bible says *'and the messenger of Jehovah appeareth unto him, and saith unto him, `Jehovah [is] with thee, O mighty one of valour.'* The Hebrew word for valour is 'chayil' which literally means *'strength, might, ability, wealth, force and part of an army'* And so it will be with you disciple of Christ. JEHOVAH is with you and because he is with you, you are an end time 'Mighty One of valour filled with the Strength of God, the Might of God, the power of God and the wealth of God, part of the end times force and army of God'

Gideon was delivered from an evil mentality by the grace of God. The Israelites did evil in the sight of JEHOVAH, and were bound and held captive to the Midianites, ***Judges 6:1 'Then the children of Israel did evil in the sight of the LORD'*** because Israel did evil, here we see what the consequences were, the enemy came in to steal, kill and destroy, which are a type of unclean spirits in the New Testament! ***Judges 6:3-6 "So it was, whenever Israel had sown, Midianites would come up; also Amalekites and the people of the East would come up against them. Then they would encamp against them and destroy the produce of the earth as far as Gaza, and leave no sustenance for Israel, neither sheep nor ox nor donkey. For they would come up with their livestock and their tents, coming in as numerous as locusts; both they and their camels were without number; and they would enter the land to destroy it. So Israel was greatly impoverished because of the Midianites, and the children of Israel cried out to the Lord."*** Before JEHOVAH delivered Gideon, he was threshing wheat in a winepress in order to hide it from the Midianites. He didn't know who he was, he was living in fear, he was bound to the Midianites, he was living in poverty, he was living in his natural circumstance, outside of his **KINGDOM** identity and how **JEHOVAH** saw him, and created him to be! Gideon eventually realized who he was, once he realized who God was after a series of miracles, mighty signs and wonders revealed to Gideon through fire, a fleece and the **ANGEL** of the LORD '*Judges 6:21-22 "fire rose out of the rock and consumed the meat and the unleavened bread. And the Angel of the Lord departed out of his sight. Now Gideon perceived that He was the Angel of the Lord. So Gideon said, "Alas, O Lord God! For I have seen the Angel of the Lord face to face."* Gideon still living in fear, doubt and unbelief asked **JEHOVAH** for more Signs! '*Judges 6:36-40 "So Gideon said to God, If You will save Israel by my hand as You have said— look, I shall put a fleece of wool on the threshing floor; if there is dew on the fleece only, and it is dry on all the ground, then I shall know that You will save Israel by my hand, as You have*

272

said. And it was so. When he rose early the next morning and squeezed the fleece together, he wrung the dew out of the fleece, a bowlful of water. Then Gideon said to God, Do not be angry with me, but let me speak just once more: Let me test, I pray, just once more with the fleece; let it now be dry only on the fleece, but on all the ground let there be dew. And God did so that night. It was dry on the fleece only, but there was dew on all the ground' And so it is with you; JEHOVAH has appeared to you; and revealed to you, who you are in the KINGDOM of God and his WORD! He revealed your KINGDOM identity as an end time 'Mighty one of valour' called to the deliverance Ministry and called to be a deliverer like Gideon! He has shown you miracles, Mighty signs and healing wonders to get your attention and he spoke his divine IDENTITY over you by his WORD! You have the strength, ability, might, and wealth of God to fulfill your destiny in the Christ! *I want to encourage you to tenaciously go hard after who God has called you to be!*

You cannot lose because **JEHOVAH; JESUS** and the Holy Ghost are with you, like they were with Gideon! Always remember the Holy Ghost is **ORCHESTRATING** your deliverance as your intimacy, fellowship, and communion with him goes to the next level. *I am praying for you; that you will be unstoppable for the KINGDOM of God, fulfilling the DESTINY he has for you in the perfect will of God! 'Going in the NAME of him who CONQUERED all, 'Jesus Christ.'*

Please visit our website for resources, sermons, teachings, and contact info.

Please write us and let us know how this book blessed you. email address: peter.valenzuela@expandmykingdom.com

Sincerely

deliverance evangelist,

Peter Valenzuela,

EXPAND MY KINGDOM

evangelistic association 2024

ABOUT THE AUTHOR

Peter Valenzuela is a missionary evangelist to Africa, Mexico and India, a deliverance evangelist, teacher, preacher, author, pastor, and Co-founder of **EXPAND MY KINGDOM** evangelistic association. Bro Peter was born in **PHX AZ** in 1975 and was born again in 2008 after seeing the divine Master Jesus Christ face to face at the **PHX** dream center.

Peter's mandate, and mantle is to equip believers to live in the **KINGDOM** of God and crush the satanic kingdom! Bro Peter has 6 beautiful children, Joshua, Brandon, Sarah, Israel, Aliza and Jadon. And 2 grandchildren Reign and Royal. When he is not preaching the Gospel; he is an entrepreneurial Sales rep for a successful packaging firm. His hobbies include writing, working out, hiking, playing sports with his boys, listening to music, fitness and mountain bike riding!

EVANGELIST PETER VALENZUELA

Suggested readings and books referenced or cited in "DELIVERANCE"

Derek Prince – They shall expel demons *(referenced in Chapter 1, the battle between two kingdoms, the Clash between two kingdoms)* **Frank and Ida Mae Hammond** – Pigs in the Parlor, Praise a weapon of warfare *(referenced in Chapter 8 love is the foundation for deliverance, Chapter 10, praise brings triumph over demon powers)* **Pablo Botarri** Free in Christ *(referenced in the 7 steps to freedom Chapter 9)* **Michael W Smith** - Planos spirits *(referenced in Can a Christian have demons, Chapter 7)* **Lester Sumrall** - Demons and deliverance sermon series *(referenced in Chapter 4 what is deliverance)* **TL Osborn** – Healing the Sick *(referenced in chapter 10 Confession,)* **EW Kenyon** – Jesus the Healer, A new kind of love *(referenced in Chapter 8 love is the foundation for deliverance)* **Monty Mulkey** - The Pearl of Great price *(referenced in Gods elite, what is deliverance Chapter 4)* **Chester and Betsy Kylstra** – Biblical healing and deliverance *(referenced in the 7 steps to freedom, ungodly beliefs, Godly beliefs Chapter 9)* **Win Worley** – Battling the host of hell series. **David Middleton** – deliverance for all Christians *(referenced in deliverance in the Old Testament Chapter 4)* **Carlos Annacondia** - *Listen to me Satan.*

EVANGELIST PETER VALENZUELA

Made in the USA
Columbia, SC
26 October 2024

44786305R00152